501 Amazing Uses for Salt, Vinegar, Baking Soda, Olive Oil & Lemons

501
Amazing Uses
for Salt,
Vinegar,
Baking Soda,
Olive Oil
& Lemons

Laura M. Westdale

Thunder Bay
P·R·E·S·S

THUNDER BAY
P · R · E · S · S

Thunder Bay Press
An imprint of Printers Row Publishing Group
A division of Readerlink Distribution Services, LLC
10350 Barnes Canyon Road, Suite 100, San Diego, CA 92121
www.thunderbaybooks.com

Printers Row Publishing Group is a division of Readerlink Distribution Services, LLC.
Thunder Bay Press is a registered trademark of Readerlink Distribution Services, LLC.

All notations of errors or omissions should be addressed to Thunder Bay Press, Editorial Department, at the above address. All other correspondence (author inquiries, permissions) concerning the content of this book should be addressed to:
powerHouse Packaging & Supply, Inc.
37 Main Street • Brooklyn, NY • 11201
info@powerhousepackaging.com

Library of Congress Cataloging-in-Publication Data:
Westdale, Laura M.
501 amazing uses for salt, vinegar, baking soda, olive oil, and lemons/ Laura M. Westdale.
208 pages cm
Includes bibliographical references and index.
ISBN 978-1-62686-067-4 (alk. paper) -- ISBN 1-62686-067-X (alk. paper)
1. Spices. 2. Food additives. I. Title. II. Title: Five hundred-one amazing uses for salt, vinegar, baking soda, olive oil, and lemons.
TX406.W47 2013
641.6'383--dc23
2013035957

Design and illustrations by J. Longo

Printed in Malaysia
21 20 19 18 17   4 5 6 7 8

CONTENTS

INTRODUCTION:
The Natural Home

If you're like most of us, you probably have numerous half-used containers of household and personal products stashed under the kitchen and bathroom sinks, in the laundry room, the garage, and the basement. These formulas are often costly, loaded with toxic and/or untested substances, evil-smelling or overly perfumed, intended for just a single task, over-packaged, and in many cases, not even all that effective. Get rid of them! You don't need all those products to keep your home, garden, and family healthy and in good working order—most of the items you need are probably already in your pantry. Separately and together, natural, non-toxic substances such as salt, vinegar, baking soda, olive oil, and lemon juice can do almost anything commercially made products can do—and they are healthy, kind to the environment, and much better-smelling.

This book contains more than 500 household hints and solutions that use these five main ingredients to accomplish a wealth of tasks—all are earth-friendly, versatile, natural, healthy, easy to make, and simple to use.

Read on to find out what makes these home helpers so effective—or just turn to the formulas and get started!

Why Salt?

Salt, or sodium chloride (NaCl), is the chemical combination of two elements, sodium and chloride. Sodium chloride is crystalline in form and typically ranges from white to pink, gray, or light brown in color.

Salt is the most common nonmetallic mineral in the world; it is found naturally in the ocean, as well as in underground and underwater salt deposits all over the world. Salt has even been found on Mars!

SALT IN HISTORY

For thousands of years, salt was a rare and precious commodity. No one has summed up the influence of salt better than Mark Kurlansky in his book, *Salt: A World History*: "salt has influenced the establishment of trade routes and cities, provoked and financed wars, secured empires, and inspired revolutions." In Ancient Rome, the Roman legions received a portion of their pay as *salarium argentum*, or money intended to purchase salt (the origin of the word "salary"). The first of the great Roman roads was the Via Salaria, the Salt Road. Salt's value means that it has been taxed through the ages, from the Chinese Emperor Hsia Yu in 2200 BCE to Charles of Anjou in medieval France; salt taxes inspired riots in Russia in 1648 and protests in India in 1930.

Salt has thousands of uses, from personal to industrial and commercial, though this book will focus on those you can employ to enhance your life. Salt's most prominent use since ancient times has been as a seasoning. After all, it's considered a primary taste that our brains are hard-wired to perceive. Almost every food is improved by the addition of salt. Since this is not a cookbook, however, the kitchen tips you will find here are for using salt to enhance your cooking methods and your experiences in the kitchen.

Salt's next most important property is its ability to preserve food. Spoilage is caused by molds, fungi, bacteria, and enzymes that break down the tissues in your food. Salting food inhibits this microbial growth in a number of ways, and has been a traditional method of preserving both meat and vegetables for thousands of years.

Around the house, salt has a number of properties that make it especially useful as a cleaning agent. Undissolved (i.e., dry) salt is a mild abrasive, perfect for scrubbing without scratching. It also has some absorbent properties. Dissolved in water, salt becomes a saline solution, able to tackle a number of protein-based stains, including blood and perspiration.

Its antiseptic properties make salt an invaluable agent for cleaning, disinfecting, and purifying. Ancient healers also knew its value, and salt can be used for health, hygiene, and personal care. In the green home, salt is an essential ingredient, the foundation of many formulas and the basis of hundreds of helpful tips.

> **"Of all smells, bread; of all tastes, salt."**
> — George Herbert, English poet (1593-1633)

TYPES OF SALT

Unrefined salt is harvested or mined from natural sources and has not been processed in any way, so it includes all the trace elements that make up salt in nature. Refined salt has been through an industrial process to remove all these elements, so it is pure sodium chloride.

Sea Salt Containing trace amounts of clays and minerals specific to the region where they are produced, these unrefined salts are ideal for cooking. There are sea salts from many regions worth trying.

Table Salt This common form of processed salt is enriched with iodine (necessary for thyroid health) as well as anti-caking agents that prevent clumping. It is ideal for household purposes, and can be used in all of the formulas in this book unless another type is specified.

Rock Salt Halite, or rock salt, is a mined salt that hasn't been purified. It is not used to season food, but food-grade rock salt has other kitchen uses.

Epsom Salt Not truly a salt, Epsom salt is a mineral compound made of magnesium, sulfur, and oxygen.

Kosher Salt Mined and left unprocessed, Kosher salt is known for its large, irregularly shaped flakes. Kosher salt is often preferable to regular table salt in food preparation.

In this book, unless a particular salt is recommended, regular table salt may be used.

Why Vinegar?

Vinegar is a substance that contains water, acetic acid, and a variety of other components, depending on what it was made from. Typically, vinegar is made from fruits, grains, or even vegetables. Vinegar is produced by a double action of fermentation—sugars are converted to alcohol and then to acetic acid. For example, in malt vinegar, the yeasts in the grain convert its sugars into alcohol by fermentation, then a kind of bacteria called acetobacter converts the alcohol to acetic acid.

Historically and today, vinegar has numerous uses as a preservative, a condiment, a healing agent, and a cleanser. Vinegar has demonstrated anti-bacterial properties, and is useful as a solvent. Its main component is acetic acid, of which most commercial vinegars contain approximately 5 percent. Because of its acidic nature, it has a very long shelf life and does not require refrigeration.

501 AMAZING USES FOR SALT, VINEGAR, BAKING SODA, OLIVE OIL & LEMONS

VINEGAR IN HISTORY

Vinegar was widely used in ancient times, and is old enough that its origins are quite lost, though many historians assume that soured wine was the first source. Its name comes from the French words for wine, *vin*, and sour, *aigre*. It likely was discovered by different civilizations independently at different times. Vinegar is mentioned in Babylonian scrolls that date as far back as 5000 BCE; evidence of vinegar was found in Egyptian urns from approximately 3000 BCE. The ancient Greek physician Hippocrates used vinegar to treat a variety of ailments including ulcers, while Pliny the Elder recounts in his *Natural History* (77–79 CE) the tale of Cleopatra's famous bet that she could consume a fortune in just one meal, in which she dissolves a pearl in a glass of vinegar and drinks it. Ancient Roman soldiers drank a vinegar concoction called *posca*. Hannibal is said to have used vinegar to dissolve boulders as he crossed the Alps in 218 BCE. In the ancient East, mention of vinegar can be found in the *Zuo Zhuan*, an early Chinese history from the fourth century BCE; vinegar-making techniques had found their way to Japan by the fourth century CE. Biblical references to vinegar reveal its use in the kitchen and the sickroom; by the Middle Ages, vinegar was in common use for numerous purposes from pickling to cleaning, and was produced commercially.

As a household cleaner, vinegar is marvelously versatile, and may be used safely on a wide variety of surfaces and materials from wood and tile to fabric. It is an excellent deodorizer, and though it has a strong odor fresh from the bottle, the distinctive sour smell soon fades completely. Vinegar dissolves all kinds of deposits and lifts stains. Best of all, it is completely non-toxic.

Vinegar has a long history of use in healing, and home remedies containing vinegar are useful against many minor complaints, from sore throats to irritated skin. Studies are ongoing to discover how vinegar may affect the regulation of blood sugar and cholesterol, and whether it can help treat ailments such as arthritis, cystitis, and diabetes.

There are also many cosmetic and personal hygiene uses for vinegar, from facial toning to hair clarifying.

> **"It is better to be preserved in vinegar than to rot in honey."**
> —Old proverb, cited in Ebenezer Cobham Brewer's *Dictionary of Phrase and Fable*, 1895

TYPES OF VINEGAR

Vinegar is made from a wide range of fruits, grains, and vegetables—any food item that contains sugar. That means there are numerous kinds of vinegar, but the most common varieties include:

Apple cider vinegar: Made from apples, apple cider vinegar varies in color from pale to dark yellow- brown, and is used both in cooking and home remedies.

Balsamic vinegar: A specialty of the Emilia-Romagna region of Italy, this is a sweet, dark vinegar much prized in cooking.

Malt vinegar: Made from malted barley, malt vinegar has a rich, full-bodied flavor and is mostly used as a condiment.

Rice vinegar: Sweet and mild compared to grape-based vinegars, rice vinegars are made from fermented rice or rice wine; they are a staple of Asian cuisine.

White vinegar: The most common kind of vinegar for household uses, white vinegar (which is actually clear) is typically made from corn alcohol. It is also called distilled vinegar.

Wine vinegar: Made from red or white wines (starting with grapes, of course), these sharp-flavored vinegars are used in cooking.

In this book, white vinegar is commonly recommended for cleaning purposes; for cooking, specific vinegars are recommended. If no particular type of vinegar is suggested, use white vinegar.

Why Baking Soda?

Baking soda, aka sodium bicarbonate, is made from combining two natural substances, sodium hydroxide and carbonic acid. Baking soda is found in nature as a substance called nahcolite, mined from an ore called trona, but most baking soda in use today is manufactured rather than mined. Though natural baking soda is crystalline in form, the baking soda we purchase in stores and use in our homes is a white powder.

"Signor Lassparri comes from a very famous family. His mother was a well-known bass singer. His father was the first man to stuff spaghetti with bicarbonate of soda, thus causing and curing indigestion at the same time."
—Groucho Marx, American comedian (1890-1977)

BAKING SODA IN HISTORY

Though baking soda in its natural form may have been used as a cleaning agent in ancient Egypt, there is no real evidence of its use in baking until more modern times. Until the advent of baking soda, bakers had typically used other methods of leavening, such as prolonged kneading or adding yeast. When it was discovered that potash, a substance made from dry hardwood ashes, made dough rise faster, people began looking for ways to develop a better chemical leavening agent.

One of these was a French chemist named Nicolas LeBlanc, who in 1791 was awarded a patent by the French government for his eponymous process for converting sea salt to soda ash, creating sodium bicarbonate. When heated, sodium bicarbonate releases carbon dioxide, causing batter to expand or rise. Two New York bakers, Austin Church and John Dwight, started a factory in 1846 to produce baking soda; their business eventually became Arm & Hammer.

In 1861, Ernest Solvay, a Belgian chemical engineer, came up with the Solvay process, which is still in use today. Though naturally derived baking soda can be procured, most readily availible product is manufactured.

As its name implies and its history attests, baking soda is largely associated with cooking, and its main use is as a leavener—though, as you will see in this book, it has many other uses. Baking soda is mildly alkaline, and can be used to neutralize acids, which makes it useful in places ranging from the lab to the medicine cabinet. An effective antacid, it is often prescribed for cases of indigestion. Baking soda has other healing properties, including soothing irritated skin and insect bites.

Around the house, baking soda is an excellent cleaning agent, with mild abrasive properties. It acts as a very effective deodorizer, stain lifter, and polishing agent. For personal use, baking soda is a versatile ingredient that can be used in toothpaste, baths, and even as an aftershave.

TYPES OF BAKING SODA

Unlike the other ingredients in this book, there is really just one type of baking soda, which is easily purchased at the supermarket.

Why Olive Oil?

Olive oil is made by extracting the oil from the fruit of the olive tree (*Olea europeaea*). Wild olive trees are native to the lands of Asia Minor, where their fruit was likely collected by ancient peoples many thousands of years ago. Cultivation of olive trees is thought to have begun in the eastern Mediterranean basin, possibly as early as the Bronze Age, some 4500 years ago.

In North America, olive oil is known primarily for its utility in cooking (a phrase that really does not do justice to olive oil's sublime flavor) but it also has plenty of uses in personal care, natural remedies, home maintenance, and cleaning.

Olive oil possesses fatty acids and polyphenols that are thought to be responsible for many of its health benefits, which include cholesterol regulation and anti-inflammatory effects. It may have a protective effect against certain forms of cancer, and may also be helpful against hypertension and in the maintenance of healthy levels of blood sugar.

For personal hygiene, olive oil has multiple uses, particularly cleansing and moisturizing, but it can also be used for shaving, hair care, and even healing. It is an excellent moisturizer and skin protector. It's good for pets, too! A little bit added to

"The olive tree is surely the richest gift of heaven."
—Thomas Jefferson, American politician (1743-1826)

your pet's dry food will not only make it taste better, but it will also give your pet the same health benefits it offers humans.

Around the home, olive oil can be useful in furniture care, maintenance of kitchen and garden equipment, and small repair jobs.

OLIVE OIL IN HISTORY

Olive oil features mightily in the history of the Mediterranean. Cultivation of olive trees may have begun in the 8th millenium BCE, and archaeologists have unearthed olive oil amphorae dating back to 3500 BCE. Mention of olives and olive oil is common in ancient Western literature, from Homer through the Bible and beyond. For the ancient Greeks, olive trees were a gift from the goddess Athena, and olive oil was used for religious rituals, in medicine, for personal hygiene, in cooking, and as fuel. Hippocrates suggested it for numerous ailments; Olympian athletes received amphorae of olive oil as a reward for their feats. The conquering Romans spread the olive across Europe and northern Africa, and around the first century CE, Pliny mentions the excellent quality and prices of Italian olive oil. In the sixteenth century, explorers brought olive trees to the New World.

Today, Spain, Italy, and Greece are the three largest producers of olive oil, accounting for about 75 percent of world production.

TYPES OF OLIVE OIL

Olive oil is expressed from olives; first the olives are made into a paste, then the oil is extracted through pressing or in a centrifuge. "Virgin" means that the oil has been pressed and produced without the use of chemicals; "refined" means that chemicals have been used in producing the oil.

Extra Virgin Olive Oil (EVOO): The highest quality, lowest in acidity, fruity and resplendent with the flavors of the land where the olive trees grew (a quality known as *terroir*), EVOO is ideal for use in salads and recipes where the flavor of the olive oil is important. "Cold-pressed" means that no heat was used in making the oil.

Virgin Olive Oil: This is not refined but usually less intensely flavorful than EVOO. Virgin olive oil is an excellent choice for cooking, particularly sautéing or frying; it is also good for personal use.

Olive Oil: A blend of virgin and refined oil; good for cooking, personal use, or household tasks.

Olive Pomace Oil: Pomace is what is left over after the oil has been pressed out of the olive; it yields small amounts of olive oil that are usually blended with refined oil to create the final product.

Lampante: Oil that is not fit for consumption but is used for oil-burning lamps and industrial purposes.

There are further distinctions seen on labels, such as "light," but these are not regulated and usually refer to taste, not calories.

Why Lemons?

Lemons are citrus fruits that grow on trees in warm (subtropical) climates. They have a yellow rind, a white pith, and an acidic inner pulp with a sour taste. The juice of the lemon is about 5 percent citric acid. Citric acid, lemon oil, and pectin are the main byproducts of lemons.

LEMONS IN HISTORY

Lemons likely originated in Southeast Asia, a hybrid of the lemon-like fruit known as a citron. Historical evidence suggests that lemons found their way along ancient trade routes to the Middle East and then Europe by the first century CE. The earliest mention of a lemon tree in historical literature is found in an Arabic farming treatise from the tenth century, and we know that lemons were cultivated in Italy by the fifteenth century. At first they may have been largely ornamental, with lemon trees planted in gardens throughout the Middle East. Columbus brought them to the New World; in the 1700s, Scottish physician James Lind discovered that lemons could prevent scurvy. By the nineteenth century lemon orchards were planted in Florida and California; today, most lemons come from the United States and Italy, with Spain, Greece, Turkey, Argentina, and Lebanon supplying the rest. Lemons must be picked by hand.

There are numerous uses for lemons around the home, particularly in the kitchen, where lemons are invaluable both in cooking and cleaning. Lemons have antiseptic and preservative properties; they can deodorize, bleach, and disinfect. Very high in Vitamin C, or ascorbic acid, lemons and lemon juice have healthful effects as well, and are used to aid digestion and healing, as well as in aromatherapy. Lemons also have many uses in beauty and hygiene, not only for their acidic properties but also for their scent, making lemon juice a sought-after ingredient in products from perfume to hair stylers.

TYPES OF LEMONS

Bottled lemon juice may be used in most of the formulas in this book. For cooking, fresh lemon juice is always preferred.

Eureka: The most common lemon found at North American supermarkets, the Eureka originated in California (from Italian seeds) and is commercially grown there and in other coastal climates. Its fruits are medium-skinned, juicy, and have fewer seeds than the Lisbon.

Lisbon: The Lisbon originally comes from Australia (probably from seeds originating in Portugal). It is a vigorous, thorny tree that produces a juicy, highly acidic lemon with a slightly rougher rind than the Eureka.

Meyer: Discovered in 1908 by Frank Meyer, this lemon is actually a cross between a lemon and a mandarin or orange. It has a thinner rind and is much prized by cooks for this reason, as well as its sweetness and aroma.

1. LIFT RED WINE STAINS

Red wine spilled on light-colored upholstery or rugs does not have to mean disaster if you tackle it swiftly. Blot the liquid and immediately pour salt directly onto the red wine stains: cover completely and pat it gently into the stain. Add a little bit of water (carbonated may be better than flat), and let dry to a crust. Vacuum or launder. The stain will be lifted, if not completely, then significantly.

2. CONDITION WICKER

- ¼ cup (60 mL) salt
- 1 cup (250 mL) warm water

A good way to keep wicker furniture clean and prevent yellowing is to scrub it with a stiff brush that you have dipped in a warm saltwater solution. Be careful not to soak the wicker; dampening it is sufficient. Let dry outdoors in the bright sunshine.

3. BRIGHTEN BRASS

Brass hardware and decorative objects may get tarnished or stained from dirt or even the oils on your hands. Make brass gleam by applying a gentle scrubbing paste made from equal parts salt, vinegar, and flour. Use a clean, soft cloth to apply, gently rub away stains, and then dry completely.

4. CLEAN STAINLESS STEEL

- 1 tablespoon (15 mL) salt
- 1 teaspoon (5 mL) lemon juice

Make a paste; apply to stainless surfaces with a soft cloth. Wipe clean.

5. CLEAN A STICKY IRON

To keep the pressing surface of your iron smooth and free of residue, pour salt onto a piece of paper and iron it until the bottom of your iron is completely clean.

6. PRESERVE BROOM BRISTLES

A new straw broom will last longer if you soak it in salty water for 20 minutes then let dry completely before using it.

7. PREVENT FROST FROM FORMING INSIDE WINDOWS

An overnight freeze can leave a layer of frost over your windows. Stop it from forming by wiping your windows, inside and out, with a solution of 1 part salt to 8 parts water applied with a clean, lint-free cloth.

8. KEEP LINE-DRIED CLOTHING FROM FREEZING

If you are going to line-dry clothing in the cold weather, add a small amount of salt to the final rinse cycle. It will prevent the items from freezing.

9. CLEAN AND BRIGHTEN A FADED RUG

- 1 cup (250 mL) salt

- 2 cups (500 mL) warm water

A salt-water sponge-bath is a gentle way to bring an old rug back to life. Mix salt into the warm water. Dip a sponge or cloth into the solution and lightly wipe it over the faded spots. Do not soak the rug! A light wipe will do the trick.

10. LIFT PERSPIRATION STAINS

- 1 tablespoon (15 mL) salt

- 1 cup (250 mL) water

Dissolve the salt in a bucket or basin of tepid water and soak freshly sweaty clothing for an hour to lift stains before they settle. Launder as usual.

11. RESTORE COPPER'S SHINE

Like other soft metals, including brass, bronze, and pewter, copper can become stained with regular use. Make it shine again with a solution of equal parts salt and vinegar. Make a paste, apply it with a soft cloth, gently rub, rinse thoroughly, and dry completely.

12. LAY OUT AN ANT BARRIER

To deter ants, try spreading a line of salt about ⅛ inch (3 mm) thick along window ledges and doorways where ants commonly enter.

13. DRIP-PROOF CANDLES

- 2 tablespoons (30 mL) salt
- enough water to cover

Soak tapers in this strong saltwater solution for 2 hours, then let dry completely before using to lessen wax dripping.

501 AMAZING USES FOR SALT, VINEGAR, BAKING SODA, OLIVE OIL & LEMONS

14. DE-FLEA PET BEDS

Salt is not friendly to fleas. Sprinkle it liberally on freshly washed pet bedding, let stand overnight, then vacuum it up. To be safe, throw out the vacuum bag or empty the tank.

15. DISCOURAGE FLEAS IN CARPETS AND RUGS

If you are worried that fleas may have jumped from your pet to your rugs, cover the rugs with a layer of salt and leave it on overnight. Vacuum thoroughly in the morning, then dispose of the bag or clean the tank.

16. DEODORIZE THE VACUUM BAG

Kill odors in a vacuum cleaner by sprinkling salt generously inside the bag or tank.

17. DE-ICE SIDEWALKS AND PATHS

A thorough sprinkling of rock salt will melt the ice that accumulates on sidewalks and paths. In a pinch, coarse table salt will melt a thin layer of ice and make it less slippery, but it's not ideal.

18. CLEAN A SLOW DRAIN

- ½ cup (125 mL) salt
- 1 gallon (4 L) hot water

Pour the salt down the drain, followed by the (very) hot water.

19. REMOVE WATER STAINS FROM WOOD

You can get rid of those unsightly white rings by mixing a paste of salt and water, and gently rubbing away the water mark. Apply a few drops of olive oil afterward to restore the shine.

20. UNCLOG A DRAIN

- 1 cup (250 mL) salt
- 1 cup (250 mL) baking soda
- ½ cup (125 mL) white vinegar
- 2 quarts (2 L) boiling water

Mix salt and baking soda thoroughly, and pour down the drain. Then add the vinegar and let it foam. 10 minutes later slowly pour the boiling water down the drain (unless you have plastic pipes, in which case, use hot water).

21. FRESHEN AN OLD SPONGE

- ¼ cup (60 mL) salt
- 1 quart (1 L) water

Soak a stinky sponge overnight in a saltwater solution and it will be clean and fresh in the morning.

22. CLEAN SHOWER DOORS

Get rid of film and cloudy residue on shower doors using a paste of equal parts salt and baking soda. Gently rub until shower doors are clear again. Spritz with white vinegar and wipe clean for extra sparkle.

23. SCRUB THE TUB

- 6 tablespoons (90 mL) coarse salt
- 2 tablespoons (30 mL) lemon juice

Make a paste and apply with sponge or cleaning cloth.

24. SCOUR THE TOILET

- ¼ cup (60 mL) salt
- 1 cup (250 mL) baking soda

Mix the salt and baking soda together. Use a sponge to clean the toilet seat, rim, and base, instead of a commercial powder cleanser.

25. MAKE YOUR OWN FOAMING TOILET CLEANSER

- ¼ cup (60 mL) salt
- 1 cup (250 mL) baking soda
- 1 ½ cups (380 mL) white vinegar

Pour all three ingredients into the toilet and, as the formula foams, use your toilet brush to scrub the bowl.

26. ELIMINATE STAINS IN THE TOILET BOWL

Stains may be caused by rust or mineral deposits, among other things. You don't need a harsh chemical cleaner to get rid of them—try salt instead. Shut off the water valve and flush to empty the toilet of water. Sprinkle a generous amount of salt on the stain. Let sit 10 minutes, then scrub with a stiff brush or non-abrasive pad.

27. DEODORIZE DIRTY LAUNDRY

- 1 cup (250 mL) white vinegar

A load of laundry filled with stinky socks and other similarly odoriferous items may not emerge smelling quite as clean as you would like. Boost the deodorizing effect by adding a cup of vinegar. You can add it at the beginning with the detergent, or even more effectively, as the final rinse cycle is filling.

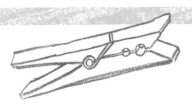

28. KEEP LINE-DRIED CLOTHING SOFT

- ¼ cup (60 mL) to 2 cups (500 mL) white vinegar

If you are putting the clothes out to dry on the line, add vinegar to the rinse cycle to keep them from getting stiff as they dry. For a small load of clothing, a quarter cup (60 mL) will do; for a larger load of household linens, for example, you may want to add more.

29. BRIGHTEN COLORS

- ½ cup (125 mL) white vinegar

Vinegar can also brighten the fading colors of your clothing and linens. Repeated laundering can fade colors due to accumulation of detergent residue; vinegar strips it away, leaving your colors brighter. Add to the rinse cycle when the water is half to full.

30. FRESHEN PILLOWS

- 1 cup (250 mL) white vinegar

Even protected by cases, pillows absorb everything from sweat to hair products, and they can lose their freshness quickly. Every 3 months, launder your pillows, adding white vinegar to thoroughly clean and eliminate any odors; it will leave them smelling fresh.

31. BRIGHTEN RUGS

Use white vinegar to wet a rag (it should be wet but not dripping) and wrap it around the bristles of your broom. Use this to vigorously sweep a faded or tired looking rug and restore the vividness of its colors.

32. PREVENT PUPPY PEE

A mixture of equal parts white vinegar and water in a spray bottle will help you teach your puppy not to pee on the rug. Spray it lightly over the entire rug; if puppy has already had an accident, apply the mixture directly to the spot and rub until no urine odor is left. Keep it handy and spray regularly until puppy is trained.

33. LIFT RUG STAINS

- 1 tablespoon (15 mL) white vinegar
- 1 tablespoon (15 mL) cornstarch

Make a paste and apply it thickly to the stain, then let dry for 48 hours. Vacuum up the dried paste.

34. ERASE FRIDGE SPILLS

Spills in the refrigerator can lead to odors. Clean and deodorize your fridge with a solution of 1 part vinegar and 1 part warm water, applied to a clean cloth. Wipe all surfaces.

35. CLEAN INSIDE THE DISHWASHER

Though the dishwasher is a cleaning appliance, it can get dirty, and benefits from a monthly wipe-down to eliminate stains and detergent build-up, and to disinfect. Simply soak a sponge or cloth in full-strength white vinegar and use it to firmly wipe the inside walls and baskets of the dishwasher, paying special attention to corners and crevices where germs can lurk.

36. AVOID DETERGENT DEPOSITS

Once a month, pour white vinegar into your dishwasher's rinse dispenser before you run a load. It will reduce mineral deposits and soap build-up.

37. DE-STAIN A COFFEE MAKER

A solution of 2 parts vinegar to 1 part water will restore a stained coffeemaker to a pristine state. Pour the mixture into the reservoir and run the machine; let stand. After about 20 minutes, pour it out, then run the machine again using plain water to eradicate any lingering vinegar scent.

38. CLEAN YOUR KETTLE

- ½ cup (125 mL) vinegar
- 2 cups (500 mL) water

Eliminate build-up in your kettle by boiling this mixture for about 10 minutes. Let it cool, then bring a kettle full of fresh water to a boil; pour it out, and then use your newly clean kettle as usual.

501 AMAZING USES FOR SALT, VINEGAR,
BAKING SODA, OLIVE OIL & LEMONS

39. CLEAR UP CLOUDY WINEGLASSES

After repeated dishwasher runs, wineglasses can become cloudy. To make them clear again, soak in full-strength white vinegar for an hour or so; rinse and wash the glasses by hand in clean, hot water, and dry thoroughly.

40. OUT WATER SPOTS

Use white vinegar in your dishwasher's rinse agent dispenser to prevent spotting on glasses.

41. MAKE WINDOWS SPARKLE NATURALLY

- 1 cup (250 mL) white vinegar
- 1 cup (250 mL) hot water

This super-simple window cleaner will leave windows streak-free. Just pour both ingredients into a spray bottle and spritz on the window. Use a lint-free cloth or crumpled newspaper to wipe the window clean.

42. MAKE A LEMON-SCENTED WINDOW CLEANER

- 1 cup (250 mL) white vinegar
- 1 cup (250 mL) warm water
- 10 to 12 drops of lemon essential oil

Remove film and grease from windows with this lemony formula. Pour the water and vinegar into a spray bottle, add the lemon oil and shake it up. Spray directly onto the window and rub with a lint-free cloth.

43. RESTORE FINE GLASS OR CRYSTAL VASES TO SPARKLING

- 1 cup (250 mL) white vinegar
- 2 or 3 drops of dish soap

Bring a cloudy vase back to a sparkling clean state by scrubbing it with this mixture. Mix the dish soap into the vinegar and soak a cleaning rag; thoroughly scrub the vase until all traces of residue are gone. Rinse with water and dry.

44. SHINE UP A MIRROR

- ⅓ cup (75 mL) white vinegar
- ⅓ cup (75 mL) cornstarch

Thoroughly combine the ingredients in a bowl. Apply to a lint-free cloth and wipe the mirror clean. You can use this same solution to wipe streaky or dirty glass in picture frames.

45. CLEAN THE TV SCREEN

To remove soot, fingerprints, and streaks, make a gentle solution of 1 part white vinegar to 10 parts warm water. Lightly dampen a clean, lint-free cloth and wipe the screen clean.

46. DEGREASE THE STOVETOP

Fill a spray bottle with equal parts vinegar and water; spray the stovetop and wipe clean.

47. SCOUR THE OVEN WITHOUT CHEMICALS

- ½ cup (125 ml) white vinegar
- 2 cups (500 mL) baking soda
- 3 drops natural dish soap
- water, as needed

In a large bowl, slowly mix the vinegar into the baking soda (it will foam). Add the soap and water, stirring to make a paste. Apply thickly to the sides and bottom of your oven, and let sit for 6 hours. Use a non-abrasive scrubber, and scour using circular motions. Wipe clean.

48. CLEAN UP A GREASY OVEN WINDOW

When your oven window gets darkened with a greasy film, make a cleaning paste from equal amounts of white vinegar and baking soda; be sure to add the vinegar slowly, as it will fizz. Cover the whole window with the paste. Let stand for at least 2 hours; wipe clean.

49. CATCH FLIES WITH VINEGAR

- 2 tablespoons (30 mL) apple cider vinegar
- 1 piece overripe fruit
- plastic wrap

Place the fruit in a glass bowl, and pour the aple cider vinegar over it. Then tightly cover the bowl with the plastic wrap, and poke a number of small holes in the wrap. Fruit flies will flock to this feast, only to find that once they are in, they can't get out again.

50. REMOVE STICKERS

Apply full-strength white vinegar to the sticker with a paintbrush or cotton ball, let stand 60 minutes, and the sticker should easily scrape off, leaving no residue.

51. REMOVE EXCESS
PAINT FROM WINDOWS

Soften any paint drips of blobs left on freshly painted windows with full-strength white vinegar. For extra power, heat it up first. Soak the paint, allow to sit for an hour, and you should find the paint to have softened enough to be easily scraped away.

52. WIPE WALLS

When it's time to give those dirty walls a cleaning, use full-strength white vinegar. It's easiest to dip a cloth into a bowl of vinegar, wring it out, then wipe the walls clean with the moist (but not dripping) cloth.

53. POLISH
PATENT LEATHER

Use a soft, clean cloth dipped in full-strength white vinegar to clean and shine up patent leather shoes or a handbag. When it is clean, buff the item to a high shine.

54. CLEAN OUT A STEAM IRON'S RESERVOIR

A steam iron can become clogged with mineral deposits. To clean it out, fill your iron's water reservoir with a mixture of 1 part white vinegar to 1 part clean water. Set to steam and allow to steam for about 5 minutes, then drain. Pour plain water into the reservoir and steam iron a rag until all traces of the vinegar are gone.

55. CLEAN WINDOW BLINDS

Wipe the slats with a one-to-one solution of white vinegar and water.

56. CLEAN SALT STAINS FROM LEATHER SHOES OR BOOTS

To make salt residue from wintry streets disappear, saturate the tip of a cotton swab with white vinegar and dab at the salt stain until it's gone. Condition the leather properly to help keep it impervious to stains.

57. CLEAN AND DEODORIZE FILTERS

The removable filters in air conditioners and humidifiers should be cleaned regularly, or at least once a season. Using a rag or soft brush, gently remove all accumulated dirt, dust, and lint, then soak the filter in a basin filled with a solution of 1 part vinegar to 1 part warm water. Let the filter soak for 30 minutes, then allow to air dry completely before reinserting.

58. ERADICATE SMOKE SMELLS

Spritz upholstery and curtains with a solution of equal parts white vinegar and water.

59. PREVENT SHOWER SLIME

Slow down the development of mold and mildew by wiping down your shower curtain or liner with full-strength white vinegar.

60. CLEAN AND DEODORIZE THE TOILET

• 2 cups (500 mL) white vinegar

Pour the vinegar into the toilet bowl, swish vigorously with toilet brush, let stand 20 minutes. Flush. You can also clean the seat and base with a sponge dipped in full-strength white vinegar.

61. ELIMINATE CALCIUM DEPOSITS ON BATHROOM FIXTURES

You can rid fixtures of mineral build-up with vinegar. Soak a rag in full-strength white vinegar and wrap it around the faucet or tap, securing with a rubber band. Let it stay there overnight, then wipe clean in the morning.

62. SHINE UP THE CHROME

Buff chrome fixtures with a cloth moistened with full-strength white vinegar.

63. DISSOLVE BATHTUB RINGS

A solution of 1 part salt to 4 parts vinegar makes an effective soap scum dissolver. Pour into a spray bottle and spray generously onto the ring. Wait 5 minutes and then wipe clean. This will also eliminate soap and dirt residue from sinks.

64. LAUNDER VINYL SHOWER CURTAINS AND LINERS

• 1 cup (250 mL) white vinegar

Place a mildewed shower curtain or liner in the washing machine with a load of rags; add detergent as usual, plus a cup of white vinegar. Use the gentle cycle. Line dry.

65. REMOVE STICKY RESIDUE FROM METAL

Eliminate sticky bits of tape or glue left on scissors or knives by wiping the blades with full-strength white vinegar on a rag.

66. DISINFECT COUNTERTOPS

Apply full-strength white vinegar with a clean sponge and let dry to deodorize and disinfect naturally.

67. DESTAIN PIANO KEYS

- ½ cup (125 mL) white vinegar
- 2 cups (500 mL) water

Mix the vinegar and water in a bowl. Dip a clean, soft cloth into the mixture and squeeze it out until there are no drips, then gently wipe a piano key. Use a second cloth to thoroughly dry off the key, then move on to the next one. Once you have done every key, leave the keyboard uncovered for 24 hours.

68. BRIGHTEN BRICKS

- 1 cup (250 mL) white vinegar
- 1 gallon (4 L) warm water

A brick patio or wall can fade with time and the accumulation of dust. To brighten your brick, use a damp mop to swab this solution onto the bricks. Do not soak them.

69. MAKE DULL WOODEN FLOORS SHINE

- 1 cup (250 mL) white vinegar
- 1 gallon (4 L) warm water

Wooden flooring can grow dull with leftover detergent or wax residues. Remove the layer of film by using a damp mop dipped in this solution and let dry.

70. DECONTAMINATE DOORKNOBS

Pour full-strength white vinegar onto a clean cloth until it is thoroughly moistened but not dripping; wipe doorknobs and handles clean.

71. DEODORIZE A WET MATTRESS

- 1 part water
- 2 parts vinegar
- baking soda

Make a solution of 1 part water to 2 parts vinegar; wet a clean rag with the solution and use it to blot the spot. Next, cover the spot with baking soda. Let dry. Vacuum.

72. DISINFECT BABY TOYS NATURALLY

Clean baby toys made of wood, rubber, or plastic with a cloth dipped in full-strength white vinegar. Air dry.

73. DUST FURNITURE

- 1 cup (250 mL) white vinegar
- ½ teaspoon (2 mL) olive oil
- 5 drops essential oil of lavender or lemon

Pour vinegar and olive oil into a spray bottle. Add essential oil. Shake well and spritz on furniture. Wipe with a lint-free cloth.

74. UNSTICK A ZIPPER

A purse or piece of luggage suffering from a stiff or stuck zipper can be remedied with a drop of olive oil applied with a cotton swab. Avoid getting oil on fabric, and do not use this method if fabric is actually caught in the zipper.

75. CLEAN AND DISINFECT WOODEN FLOORS

- ¾ cup (175 mL) olive oil
- ¼ cup (60 mL) white vinegar
- 1 gallon (4 L) water

Adding vinegar to your floor-cleaning solution provides it with disinfecting power, cuts grease, and deodorizes as well.

76. REVIVE OLD PEWTER

A few drops of olive oil applied to a darkened piece of vintage pewter with a clean, soft cloth will restore its patina without pitting or staining.

77. TOUCH UP SLATE FLOOR TILES

To transform a chalky-looking slate floor tile to a darker, richer finish, apply a small amount of olive oil with a clean cloth or rag, rubbing in completely. Repeat as needed.

78. GIVE A WOODEN FLOOR A LEMON-SCENTED SHINE

- ¾ cup (175 mL) olive oil
- ½ cup (125 mL) lemon juice
- 1 gallon (4 L) water

Mix olive oil, lemon juice, and water in a bucket; dip in a mop, wring well, and mop your floors clean. The oil will impart shine and the lemon juice brings a lovely citrus aroma.

79. RESTORE BRASS

Remove tarnish and give brass a shinier surface by lightly applying olive oil to a clean, soft cloth and wiping down the brass.

80. REMOVE CHEWING GUM FROM SURFACES

Finding a wad of old gum attached to a shoe or the underside of a piece of furniture is never fun. Soak the offensive blob with a small amount of olive oil, let stand for 5 minutes, then scrape it off with a butter knife—wrap a thin rag around the knife to prevent any of the gum adhering to the metal.

81. REMOVE STICKERS AND RESIDUE

Olive oil offers an easy, non-toxic way to remove a sticker and clean off the gooey residue it leaves behind. Simply pour a few drops onto a rag and rub the sticker, which will quickly lose its stick and ball up, allowing you to cleanly wipe away the traces.

501 AMAZING USES FOR SALT, VINEGAR, BAKING SODA, OLIVE OIL & LEMONS

82. LUBRICATE HINGES

Use a cotton swab or puff moistened with olive oil to silence squeaky door or cupboard hinges. Dab it into the hinge and wipe up any drips.

83. MAKE NON-TOXIC FURNITURE POLISH

• 2 parts olive oil to 1 part lemon juice

A protective homemade furniture polish can be made by combining olive oil and lemon juice. To use, apply a small amount to a clean, soft cloth and rub gently onto furniture with a circular motion, wiping up any excess.

84. IMPROVE THE LOOK OF SCRATCHED LEATHER

A useful but temporary fix for scratches on leather is to apply a tiny drop of olive oil with a cotton-tipped swab; be sure to remove any excess immediately.

85. WASH VEGETABLES

- 1 cup (250 mL) water
- 1 cup (250 mL) white vinegar
- 2 tablespoons (30 mL) baking soda
- 2 tablespoons (30 mL) lemon juice

Combine all ingredients in a clean spray bottle; shake. Spritz onto fresh produce and let sit 3 minutes. Scrub and rinse thoroughly under running water.

86. SOFTEN CLOTHES

- 1 teaspoon (5 mL) baking soda
- 2 cups (500 mL) cold water
- Juice of 4 lemons

Combine ingredients in a jar with a lid, close tightly, shake well, and add the formula to the rinse cycle of your washing machine.

87. CLEAN NON-STICK PANS

- 2 tablespoons (30 mL) lemon juice
- 1 teaspoon (5 mL) baking soda

Mix the lemon juice and baking soda into a paste and use it to gently scrub the pan.

88. SLIP ON RUBBER GLOVES

A few shakes of baking soda into the fingers of the gloves will make them easier to put on and take off.

89. REMOVE STAINS FROM PLASTIC

- 1 tablespoon (15 mL) lemon juice
- 1 tablespoon (15 mL) baking soda

Make a paste and scrub the stains; for tough stains, let sit 4 hours or overnight before scrubbing and rinsing clean.

BAKING SODA: THE MIRACLE DEODORIZER

Use it any- and everywhere to eliminate even the nastiest odors and make everything smell fresher and cleaner.

90. DEODORIZE THE FRIDGE
Place a box with top removed at the back of a middle shelf of the fridge; replace every two months.

91. DEORDORIZE GARBAGE PAILS AND BAGS
A few generous shakes of baking soda into the bag or can will help to prevent disgusting smells.

92. DEODORIZE RECYCLING BINS
When you replace the bag, sprinkle a light layer in the bottom of the bin.

93. DEODORIZE DIAPER PAILS
Keep this super-stinky container from becoming totally nasty by generously sprinkling baking soda in every time you open it.

94. DEODORIZE OUTDOOR GARBAGE BINS
Cover the bottom of the pail or bin in a layer of baking soda to keep smells at bay.

95. DEODORIZE LAUNDRY HAMPERS
A light sprinkle each week will keep your hamper smelling fresh despite the regular influx of dirty laundry.

96. DEODORIZE SMELLY ATHLETIC SHOES
Regular application of baking soda into athletic shoes helps prevent the growth of smelly microbes. Be sure the powder gets right up into the toe box and fully covers the insoles. Let it sit for up to a week.

97. DEODORIZE DRAWERS AND CLOSETS
A sprinkling of baking soda in the bottom of the drawer under the drawer liner or a box kept in the back of the closet is a good idea.

98. DEODORIZE RUGS AND CARPETING
In between cleanings, give your rugs and carpets a pick-me-up by sprinkling a layer of baking soda on, let it sit for 30 minutes, then vacuum it up. A light sprinkle between the rug and the rug pad can help, too.

99. DEODORIZE PET AREAS
Pet bedding will stay fresher with a regular application of baking soda; indeed, anywhere your pet hangs out can be freshened by the baking soda sprinkle-then-vacuum trick.

100. DEODORIZE YOUR LOCKER
A box in your gym locker or your child's school locker will keep it from getting musty.

101. ABOLISH OVEN SPILLS

For baked-on food, sprinkle baking soda over the bottom of the oven and then spritz it with water from a spray bottle. Let it sit overnight and then remove it in the morning with a sponge, and most of the gunk in the oven will come out with it. If baked-on spills still remain, sprinkle on some more baking soda and then add a little bit of white vinegar. Let the bubbling mixture sit for 30 minutes, and then scrub.

102. DISINFECT A STINKY SPONGE

Soak it in a bath of equal parts baking soda and vinegar for one hour.

103. CLEAN TARNISH

- 2 quarts (2 L) hot water
- 1 cup (250 mL) baking soda
- aluminum foil

Pour the water in a plastic bucket or basin, and dissolve the baking soda into it. Place a strip of tin foil at least 2 inches (5 cm) long into the water as well. Lay any tarnished silver pieces you want to clean on the bottom of basin and let it all sit for at least 30 minutes—the tarnish will vanish, leaving the silver bright and shining.

104. SCRUB THE TUB

- ¼ to ½ cup (60 mL to 125 mL) baking soda
- 1 lemon, cut in half

Sprinkle baking soda around the tub and use the cut lemon to scrub; then rinse completely.

105. SOAK STERLING SILVER JEWELRY CLEAN

- ½ cup (120 mL) white vinegar
- 2 tablespoons (30 mL) baking soda

For sterling silver jewelry (that does not contain pearls, which may be damaged by the vinegar), try this cleanser. In a large bowl, combine baking soda and vinegar. Place jewelry in the bowl and let soak for 2 hours. Wipe clean and dry.

106. SCRUB GRILL RACKS

Baking soda can help clean grill racks that are crusted with cooked-on food. Sprinkle the baking soda on a scrubbing sponge and rub down the racks until they are clean. Don't use a wire or metal brush for this purpose, as it may leave tiny shards on the rack that can get in your food.

107. CLEAN UP A CERAMIC SINK

- 1 tablespoon (15 mL) baking soda
- 2 tablespoons (30 mL) vinegar
- 1 teaspoon (5 mL) lemon juice

Make a paste of the baking soda and lemon juice, which will froth slightly. Put the paste on a sponge and lightly scour the sink; rinse with water. Then pour the vinegar into the sponge and use it to give the sink a final once-over to disinfect.

108. CLEAN STAINLESS STEEL

Stainless steel appliances suffer from fingerprints, grease, and dirt. To restore their original luster, make a paste of baking soda and water; rub it onto the stainless steel, moving with the grain. Rinse and dry, buffing to achieve a dull shine.

109. WASH THE FLOOR

- ½ cup (120 mL) baking soda
- 1 gallon (4 L) warm water

A great cleaner for no-wax floors is a simple solution of baking soda and warm water, applied with a damp mop. No need to rinse.

110. NEUTRALIZE BACTERIA ON FOOD SURFACES

Sprinkle baking soda onto food prep surfaces of any sort, such as counters, cutting boards (wooden or plastic), even stovetops, and gently scrub the entire surface to clean and disinfect; a spray of vinegar completes the sanitizing.

111. CUT GREASE IN DISHWATER

- 2 tablespoons (30 mL) baking soda

Adding baking soda to a sink filled with suds and dirty, greasy dishes will boost the cleaning power of the detergent and cut the grease.

112. BOOST LAUNDRY DETERGENT'S POWER

• ½ cup (125 mL) baking soda

Add to the laundry with your regular detergent to get your clothes their cleanest.

113. PRETREAT STAINS

Make a paste of equal parts baking soda and vinegar (it will fizz), then work it gently into the stain. Let sit for 10 minutes, then launder as usual.

114. FRESHEN UP LINENS

An open box of baking soda in the linen closet will help to keep linens smelling sweet.

115. MAKE AN ALL-PURPOSE LEMON-SCENTED CLEANER

- 3 lemon peels
- 2 cups (500 mL) white vinegar

Combine the lemon peel and vinegar in a glass jar with a tight-fitting lid. Let sit 4 weeks, shaking vigorously once or twice per week. After 4 weeks, strain through cheesecloth and pour into a spray bottle.

116. STEAM CLEAN THE MICROWAVE

Fill a medium-sized bowl with water and add half a lemon. Place in the microwave and heat on high for 2 minutes or until the water is steaming; keep the microwave door closed for 5 minutes, then remove the bowl and wipe the insides of the microwave clean.

117. CUT GREASY DISHWATER

• 2 tablespoons (30 mL) lemon juice

Add lemon juice to your dishwater to help cut the grease.

118. ELMINATE COFFEE AND TEA STAINS FROM FINE CHINA CUPS

Place a lemon wedge in a cup then fill the cup with boiling water. Soak overnight and gently wash in the morning.

119. MAKE COPPER GLEAM

• 1 fresh lemon, cut in half

• 1 tablespoon (15 mL) salt

Sprinkle the salt onto the lemon half, and use it to rub over tarnished areas. Rinse, and then completely dry.

120. BRIGHTEN ALUMINUM PANS

- 1 lemon wedge
- 3 tablespoons (45 mL) lemon juice
- 1 quart (1 L) boiling water

Boil the water and lemon for 10 minutes in the pan that has lost its luster. When it is no longer hot, rub down the outside of the pan with the lemon wedge, then rinse and dry.

121. REMOVE GARLIC AND ONION ODORS FROM HANDS

Run a fresh lemon wedge over your fingers and palms, then wash them under running water using a stainless steel spoon and a bit of dish soap.

122. FRESHEN THE GARBAGE DISPOSAL

By feeding 3 lemon rinds through the system while running cold water you can get rid of lingering odors and refresh a garbage disposal.

123. SHINE UP A STAINLESS SINK

Keep a lemon wedge handy near a stainless steel sink to impart a quick shine. After you clean the sink of any food residue and rinse it, rub down the sides with a lemon wedge to make it sparkle.

124. SHINE UP THE CHROME

Just rub it with your handy lemon wedge and dry with a soft cloth.

125. SCOUR A CUTTING BOARD

- 2 tablespoons (30 mL) lemon juice
- 2 tablespoons (30 mL) salt

Make a paste and apply it to a stained cutting board using a sponge or dishcloth. Scrub vigorously, then allow the paste to sit for 5 minutes. Rinse thoroughly and dry completely.

126. CLEAN ROLLING PINS AND WOODEN SPOONS

Rub them all over with a lemon wedge; no need to rinse.

127. PRE-TREAT SWEAT STAINS

- 1 tablespoon (15 mL) lemon juice
- 1 tablespoon (15 mL) white vinegar
- 1 cup (250 mL) water

Combine the lemon juice, vinegar, and water, and pour it directly onto the stain, making sure to saturate it. Let sit at least one hour, then wash as usual.

128. LIFT STUBBORN STAINS ON CLOTHING OR LINENS

- 1 tablespoon (15 mL) baking soda
- 1 teaspoon (5 mL) lemon juice

Sprinkle baking soda and then lemon juice on the stain and let it fizz. Rub very gently into the stain, and launder as usual.

129. BANISH MILDEW FROM A SHOWER CURTAIN

- 2 tablespoons (30 mL) lemon juice
- 1 tablespoon (15 mL) baking soda

For a tough case of shower curtain mildew, make a paste from the lemon juice and baking soda. Apply with a sponge, let stand 2 hours, and then wipe off.

130. MAKE THE FRIDGE AND FREEZER SMELL GOOD

Soak a cotton ball in lemon juice and set in fridge; wipe down the insides of the freezer with a sponge soaked in lemon juice.

131. WHITEN LINENS

- 3 cups (750 mL) lemon juice
- 1 gallon (4 L) water

Pour lemon juice and water into a large basin (or use the washing machine) and soak stained or darkened linens for 3 hours, then wring them out (or spin them) and hang to dry in the sun.

132. SWEETEN STALE INDOOR AIR

- ½ lemon

- 1 cinnamon stick

- water

Place lemon half and cinammon stick in a small pot, and add water until pot is ¾ full. Simmer on stove over low heat, adding water as needed to keep it going.

133. MAKE A SACHET

- 1 small cotton or linen bag

- 1 cup (250 mL) baking soda

- zest of 1 lemon

- 6 inches (15 cm) of ribbon

Thoroughly combine lemon zest and baking soda in a bowl, then pour the powder into the bag and tie it off tightly. Place in your linen closet or drawers for a lemon-scented sachet.

134. FRESHEN UP A HUMIDIFIER

• 1 tablespoon (15 mL) lemon juice

Pour into the basin of full humidifier and operate as usual.

135. DISSUADE ANT INTRUDERS

• zest of 3 lemons, finely chopped

Spread the lemon zest along any window ledges or doorways where ants try to enter your home.

136. BLEACH SNEAKERS

• ½ cup (120 mL) lemon juice

• 2 cups (500 mL) water

Pour lemon juice and water into a bucket or basin and soak dirty sneakers overnight. Drying them in the sun will increase the brightening power.

137. CLEAN CAST IRON PANS

- ½ cup (125 mL) salt
- ¼ cup (60 mL) vegetable oil

Rinse the skillet with hot water and scrape with a wooden spoon or non-metal spatula. Place the pan over medium heat for about 30 seconds until dry, then transfer to a cool burner. Pour in salt and oil, and then scrub with a wad of paper towels until clean. To finish, rinse again in hot water and dry over medium heat.

138. WIPE UP STOVETOP SPILLS

When splashes and spills occur as you're cooking, quickly pour salt onto the mess before it hardens. You'll be able to wipe it up later quite easily. This works inside the oven with overflows as well.

139. SMOTHER GREASE FIRES

Keep a large bowl of salt (or the delightfully old-fashioned vessel known as a "salt pig") by the stove. You'll have it handy for seasoning purposes, and it can help in the event of a grease fire. A large handful of salt poured onto the small grease fire will put out the flames swiftly. Cover it all with a pot lid to be sure it goes out.

NEVER USE WATER OR FLOUR ON A GREASE FIRE.

140. GET RID OF GREASE

Absorbent and abrasive, salt is anathema to grease. Use it to scrub greasy pots and pans by pouring it directly on the spot and rubbing with a dry sponge. Then wash as usual.

141. DEODORIZE METAL CONTAINERS

Metal water bottles can develop an odor over time; eliminate it by soaking the bottles in salty water for 10 minutes before rinsing thoroughly.

142. CHILL WINE QUICKLY

• ½ cup (125 mL) salt

• ice water

Fill a bucket or basin with ice water and add salt. Lower the wine bottle into the center up to its neck. Wait 10 minutes.

143. EASILY CLEAN DOUGH OFF SURFACES

Rolling out dough can leave a mess all over the rolling surface that is surprisingly tough to scrape up. Make it easier by covering the leftover dough with salt. Sprinkle it on and wipe up immediately.

144. REMOVE LIPSTICK SMUDGES

Lipstick marks on glasses frequently survive a trip through the dishwasher, leaving your "clean" glasses looking distinctly smudgy. A swipe of salt around the rim of the glass (use your fingers or pour onto a dishcloth) will lift off the waxy residue left by any lip product.

145. SCOUR METAL POTS AND PANS

To clean up any metal pot, make a paste of equal parts salt, white vinegar, and flour. Scrub the pot clean and rinse.

146. PREVENT GREASE SPLATTERS

A dash of salt in the frying pan before you add the oil or fat will help prevent painful grease splatters.

147. REVIVE WILTED GREENS

- 1 tablespoon (15 mL) salt
- 1 gallon (4 L) ice water

Give wilted greens or herbs an ice-water bath to revive them. Pour the water into the sink or a large bowl, add the salt, and place your greens in the salted water. Swish gently then let sit for 15 minutes. If they are not too far gone, they should perk up significantly.

148. PERK UP OLD COFFEE

A tiny pinch of salt will improve the flavor of reheated coffee. This trick also works on freshly brewed coffee—a few grains in with the grounds in the coffeemaker will counteract bitterness and improve flavor.

149. PREVENT CHEESE MOLD

A trick to help inhibit the growth of mold on cheese is to wrap the cheese in a piece of cotton cloth previously soaked in salt water.

150. WASH FRESH SPINACH

If you use lightly salted water to clean spinach, you'll find it cleans up more easily, as the salty water helps to remove the grit that tends to cling to spinach leaves. Plunge the fresh spinach into a salty bath and swish the leaves around vigorously, then triple rinse.

151. MAKE FRUIT TASTE SWEETER

Though it may seem counterintuitive, a pinch of salt makes fruit taste sweeter. Try it on summer fruits like berries and watermelon.

152. IMPROVE THE TASTE OF YOGURT

Plain yogurt can benefit from a pinch of salt, which you may find will improve the yogurt's flavor.

153. BRINE CHICKEN

- 1 cup (250 mL) kosher salt
- ¼ cup (60 mL) sugar
- 1 gallon (4 L) water

A simple poultry brine of salt and sugar will result in a moister, more flavorful chicken. Experiment with different herbs and other ingredients. Place the chicken in the brine, fully covered, and refrigerate for 4 to 6 hours (you can leave it in the brine overnight but no longer than 24 hours). Discard brine. Rinse poultry thoroughly before cooking.

154. BRINE PORK

- ¼ cup (60 mL) kosher salt
- 2 tablespoons (30 mL) sugar
- 1 quart (1 L) water

Almost any cut of pork will be improved by brining. Use 1 quart of brine per pound of meat. Immerse the meat in the brine and refrigerate for at least 1 hour and up to 8 hours. Rinse before cooking.

155. PERK UP FRESH FISH

- 1 tablespoon (15 mL) sea salt
- 2 quarts (2 L) ice cold water

Keep fish as fresh as possible before cooking by placing in icy, salty water for about 15 minutes.

156. GET A GRIP ON SLIPPERY FOOD

Before handling slippery fish or meat, sprinkle a thin layer of salt on your clean hands. It will help you to hold onto the slippery item better.

157. MAKE YOUR OWN
SIGNATURE SALT RUBS

A salt rub is a delicious way to add flavor and texture to any piece of meat, poultry, or fish. The primary ingredient is salt, plus an array of spices that you like. Simply rub the mixture on the food, and let sit for 10 to 30 minutes to season. Your own salt rub makes a great gift; present it in a jar wrapped with a ribbon and a little card with instructions for cooking.

158. MAKE A SALT
RUB FOR FISH

- 2 teaspoons (10 mL) kosher salt
- ½ teaspoon (3 mL) coarsely ground pepper
- 1 ½ teaspoons (7 mL) dried dill
- grated zest of 1 lemon

Combine ingredients and rub both sides of the fish thoroughly. Let sit for 10 minutes. Grill for approximately 10 to 15 minutes depending on thickness of fish.

159. MAKE A SALT RUB FOR STEAK

- 4 tablespoons (60 mL) coarse salt
- 1 tablespoon (15 mL) freshly ground pepper

This very simple rub brings out the best flavor in a good piece of steak. Combine the salt and pepper, then pat both sides of the meat with the rub and let sit for 10 minutes before cooking.

160. MAKE A SALT RUB FOR CHICKEN

- 3 tablespoons (45 mL) light brown sugar
- 1 tablespoon (15 mL) kosher salt
- 1 tablespoon (15 mL) dried oregano
- 1 tablespoon (15 mL) granulated garlic powder
- 1 tablespoon (15 mL) mustard powder
- 1 tablespoon (15 mL) smoked paprika
- 1 tablespoon (15 mL) chili powder

Rub evenly over entire chicken breast and let sit for 20 minutes before cooking.

161. MAKE A
SALT RUB FOR RIBS

- 1 cup (250 mL) packed dark brown sugar
- 2 tablespoons (30 mL) kosher salt
- 2 teaspoons (10 mL) smoked paprika
- 2 teaspoons (10 mL) cayenne pepper
- 2 teaspoons (10 mL) garlic powder
- 1 teaspoon (5 mL) ground allspice
- 1 teaspoon (5 mL) red pepper flakes

Ideal for pork ribs. Whisk together all ingredients in a bowl. Line a baking sheet with parchment paper and lay the ribs on it. Rub the spareribs all over with the spice rub. Cover and refrigerate for at least 2 hours and up to 6 hours before grilling.

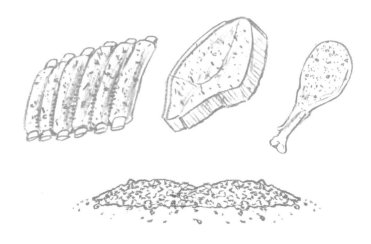

162. MAKE WHIPPED CREAM FLUFFLIER

A pinch of salt added toward the beginning of the process may help your whipped cream to whip up quicker and fluffier, as salt helps to break down the structure of the fat molecules.

163. PREPARE AN HERBED SALT FOR GRILLED VEGETABLES

- 1 cup (250 mL) sea salt
- 2 tablespoons (30 mL) herbs, fresh or dried, of your choice

Try garlic, rosemary, sage, or thyme, or a blend. Mix in blender or food processor, then sprinkle over vegetables (a light coating of olive oil will help them stick), then cook. A great homemade condiment for roasting or grilling—especially good on potatoes.

164. SALT
YOUR SWEETS

Gourmet bakers have long known that a touch of salt adds an exciting note to chocolate and caramel, intensifying flavors and enhancing the taste. Just a crystal or two of fine sea salt on a caramel or chocolate bonbon is all you need.

165. BAKE IN A SALT CRUST

- Kosher salt

- Egg whites

Salt-crust baking is an extremely simple cooking method that probably dates back to ancient times. It works particularly well for whole poultry and fish, but also for meat and vegetables. Essentially, you bury the food in a mixture of salt and egg white, which forms a hard crust all around. You'll need 2 egg whites for every cup of salt. Start by pouring a bed of the salt mixture into the bottom of a shallow roasting pan. Lay the food on it, then pack the salt mixture tightly all around. When it comes out of the oven, you crack open the shell to find a supremely delicious meal.

166. MAKE GRAVLAX

- 1 pound (500 g) fresh salmon filet
- 2 teaspoons (10 mL) sea salt
- 2 tablespoons (30 mL) sugar
- 2 slices lime
- ¾ ounce (21 g) fresh dill, chopped fine

Rinse the filet and pat dry. Place on a tray, on a sheet of plastic wrap. Combine salt and sugar then sprinkle over the fish, covering as fully as possible. Wrap the fish tightly in the plastic wrap. Place something heavy on top. Put the tray of salmon in the refrigerator for 2 to 3 days. Scrape off the seasoning. Slice and serve.

167. RIM A COCKTAIL GLASS

• Kosher, non-iodized salt or sea salt

• Wedge of lemon

Certain cocktails, notably the Margarita, the Bloody Mary, and the vodka-grapefruit juice concoction known as a Salty Dog, are dramatically enhanced by a rim of salt. Pour the salt in a saucer, then moisten the top edge of the glass all around with the lemon wedge. Upend the glass in the salt; twist and lift. Then pour in the cocktail and sip.

168. DRINK A SHOT OF TEQUILA

• Pinch of salt

• Lemon wedge

The classic method for drinking a tequila shot: pour a pinch of salt onto the back of your hand between your thumb and forefinger; lick the salt, drink the shot in one gulp; bite into the lemon wedge. One of these is sufficient for a responsible drinker.

169. MAKE PERFECT HARDBOILED EGGS

- 1 tablespoon (15 mL) white vinegar
- 3 to 6 fresh, uncracked eggs, room temperature
- water to cover

Adding vinegar when hardboiling eggs will help prevent the shells from cracking. Gently lace eggs in pot and fully cover with water. Add vinegar and bring to a boil. Let water boil for 4 minutes, then remove pot from heat and let stand 15 minutes. Run under cold water.

170. CLEAN VEGETABLES

- 1 tablespoon (15 mL) white vinegar
- cold water
- dash of salt

Soak fresh vegetables in cold water with vinegar and a bit of salt. Gently scrub off dirt and rinse clean before cooking or eating.

171. PERK UP
WILTED VEGETABLES

• 2 tablespoons white vinegar

• cold water

Vegetables that have had a long journey from the farmer's market or supermarket to your kitchen may have lost some of their vitality. Perk them by soaking them for 10 minutes in a bath of cold water laced with vinegar.

172. CORRECT AN
OVER-SALTED DISH

A teaspoon (15 mL) of white vinegar may fix a recipe if you've added too much salt. A dash of sugar may help, too.

173. MAKE
STRAWBERRIES
MORE EXCITING

Add a splash of balsamic vinegar to a bowl of fresh strawberries to enhance their flavor.

174. SOAK FISH FILETS

- 2 tablespoons (30 mL) white vinegar
- 1 quart (1 L) water

Next time you cook a fish filet, first let it marinate for 20 minutes in one quart of water and two tablespoons of vinegar. The vinegar will make it more tender while also helping the fish to hold its shape better.

175. DEGLAZE A PAN

No need to waste pan drippings when you have sauteed meat, fish, or poultry. Deglaze the pan with vinegar to make a delicious sauce. Red wine and balsamic vinegar are especially flavorful choices. Remove sauteed item and most of the fat. Combine the vinegar with wine, stock, or water, and minced shallots, if desired, adding approximately twice as much liquid as you want finished sauce. Bring to a boil, and stir and scrape the pan to get all the browned bits. When the liquid is reduced by approximately half, you are done.

176. REDUCE GAS
FROM BEANS

• 1 tablespoon (15 mL) white vinegar

To reduce the gassy effect of beans, add vinegar to the water when cooking them.

177. MAKE A MOISTER
CHOCOLATE CAKE

Add a teaspoon (15 mL) of white vinegar to the mix—whether you're making it from scratch or out of a box—to make a chocolate cake moister.

178. PREVENT COOKED
VEGETABLES FROM FADING

• 1 tablespoon (15 mL) white vinegar

When boiling or steaming vegetables, keep their colors bright by adding vinegar to the water.

A NOTE ON SAFETY

To reduce the risk for botulism when pickling, food items should be washed and cooked adequately, and utensils, containers, and other surfaces that come in contact with food, including cutting boards and hands, should be cleaned thoroughly with soap and warm water. All containers (jars and lids) in which pickling will occur should be sterilized (e.g., placed in boiling water for a prescribed period).

179. TRY HOME PICKLING

Vinegar has been used to preserve foods since ancient Roman times. Its acidic nature prevents the growth of bacteria. Before the era of refrigeration, pickling was a necessity for preserving the fruits of the harvest and for bringing food on long journeys. In the nineteenth century, two Frenchmen, the chef Nicolas Appert and the scientist Louis Pasteur (after whom the process of "pasteurization" was named) developed jars, which gave birth to the modern canning industry. Around the same time, the invention of Mason jars, with their screw-on lids and wax or rubber seals, provided an airtight seal that allowed for safer, easier home pickling.

180. REFRIGERATOR PICKLING

- 8 cups vegetables of your choice (900 g)
- 1 ½ teaspoons (8 mL) coarse salt
- 2 cups (500 mL) sugar
- 1 cup (250 mL) apple cider vinegar
- 1 teaspoon (5 mL) celery seed
- 1 teaspoon (5 mL) mustard seed

Requiring no canning equipment, refrigerator pickling is easy and delicious—and you can do this with any vegetable that you think would taste good pickled, from cauliflower to beets. In a large bowl, toss vegetables with the salt (salt draws the water from the vegetables). Set aside to drain in a colander for 30 minutes. Mix sugar, vinegar, celery seed, and mustard seed in a bowl and stir until sugar is dissolved. Divide the vegetables equally into clean jars and pour vinegar mixture over them. Tightly close jars and refrigerate at least 8 hours (and up to 2 weeks).

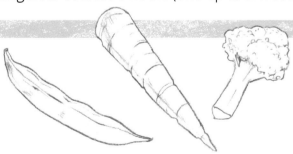

181. PICKLE EGGS

- 1 ½ cups (750 mL) apple cider vinegar
- 1 ½ cups (750 mL) water
- 1 tablespoon (15 mL) pickling spice
- 1 clove garlic, crushed
- 1 bay leaf
- 12 hardboiled eggs, shelled

In a medium saucepan, mix together the vinegar, water, and pickling spice. Bring to boil and mix in the garlic and bay leaf. Remove from heat. Transfer the eggs to sterilized glass containers with tightly fitting lids. Fill the containers with the hot vinegar mixture, seal and refrigerate for 8 to 10 days before serving. Keep refrigerated. Use within 3 months.

182. MAKE FLAVORED VINEGAR

- 1 teaspoon (5 mL) dried herbs such as thyme or tarragon

- 1 cup (250 mL) white wine or rice vinegar

Try any herb or combination you like; some nice combinations include oregano, rosemary, and marjoram. Place the herbs in a sterilized glass canning jar with a tightly fitting lid. Pour in the vinegar and seal. Store jar in a cool, dark place for 3 to 4 weeks. Using a funnel, strain the vinegar through cheesecloth into another sterilized container. Repeat as needed until all the sediment is removed and the vinegar is clear. Discard all solids and pour the strained vinegar into sterilized bottles. Keep for up to 2 months.

VINAIGRETTE

Perhaps the most perfect marriage of kitchen staples is that of vinegar and oil, as vinaigrette. The classic ratio is 1 part vinegar to 3 parts oil, but you may adjust this to taste—less vinegar yields a gentler result. The keys are quality ingredients and thorough emulsification. Try any of the following recipes or create your own.

183. CLASSIC

3 tablespoons (45 mL) extra virgin olive oil
1 tablespoons (15 mL) wine (red or white) vinegar
salt and pepper to taste

184. BALSAMIC

⅓ cup (80 mL) extra virgin olive oil
3 tablespoons (45 mL) balsamic vinegar
2 teaspoons (10 mL) Dijon mustard (optional)
salt and pepper to taste

185. TARRAGON

1 tablespoon (15 mL) lemon juice
3 tablespoons (45 mL) white wine vinegar
1 tablespoon (15 mL) Dijon mustard
1 ¼ teaspoon (6 mL) fresh tarragon, minced
1 small garlic clove, finely chopped
⅓ cup (80 mL) extra virgin olive oil

186. GARLIC DIJON

1 teaspoon (5 mL) minced fresh garlic

1 teaspoon (5 mL) Dijon mustard

3 tablespoons (45 mL) champagne vinegar

½ cup (120 mL) extra virgin olive oil

salt and pepper to taste

187. ACCORDING TO JULIA CHILD

½ tablespoon (8 mL) finely minced shallot or scallion

½ tablespoon (8 mL) Dijon mustard

¼ teaspoon (1 mL) salt

½ tablespoon (8 mL) freshly squeezed lemon juice

½ tablespoon (8 mL) wine vinegar

⅓ cup (80 mL) extra virgin olive oil

Freshly ground pepper

188. ASIAN

3 tablespoons (45 mL) rice wine vinegar

1 tablespoon (15 mL) sugar

3 tablespoons (45 mL) soy sauce

1 tablespoon (15 mL) fresh ginger, grated

½ teaspoon (3 mL) fresh garlic, minced

2 tablespoons (30 mL) sesame oil

½ cup (120 mL) canola oil

SEASON WITH A SPLASH

A splash (about a half teaspoon or 3 mL) of vinegar can enliven almost any dish. Try these different ideas:

189. Sherry vinegar in lentil soup.

190. Balsamic vinegar on a slice of melon.

191. Apple cider vinegar in cole slaw.

192. Rice vinegar over grilled vegetables.

193. Malt vinegar over French fries or other potato dishes.

194. Red wine vinegar in a simmering red sauce after you take it off the heat.

195. Toss sliced cucumbers with a splash of red wine vinegar.

196. Red wine vinegar on cooked chicken breasts.

197. Apple cider vinegar over cooked squash.

198. White wine vinegar on any bean dish.

199. Sherry vinegar over shrimp before grilling.

200. Sherry vinegar in gazpacho.

201. MAKE BUTTERMILK

You can make your own buttermilk by adding 1 tablespoon (15 mL) of white or apple cider vinegar to 1 cup (250 mL) of milk.

202. HOST A TASTING

One of the best ways to discover the range and depth of flavors in olive oil is to taste a variety of different ones—like a wine tasting. Select 3 or 4 olive oils to try. Use a clean wine glass for each. Pour in about a tablespoon (15 mL). Just as you would with wine, start by gently swirling the oil in the glass. Next inhale the aroma and think about what you are smelling. Next, slurp a small amount, swirl in your mouth, and swallow. Make notes on aroma, fruitiness, pungency, bitterness, and texture.

203. DIP BREAD

Good quality EVOO is often best enjoyed simply. Dipping a chunk of good bread into olive oil is a great way to taste it. Pour into a small bowl or ramekin. Add salt and pepper to taste, if you wish, or enjoy the pure flavor of the olive oil.

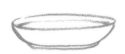  

204. LUBRICATE MEASURING EQUIPMENT

Before pouring in a sticky substance such as honey or maple syrup, wipe out the inside of your measuring cup or spoon with a very thin film of olive oil.

205. ADD FLAVOR BEFORE SERVING

Brushing or drizzling on a bit of olive oil after cooking can add a burst of rich flavor to meat or vegetables.

206. KEEP MEAT MOIST

Before grilling, brush a little olive oil over your meat to impart a dash of flavor and help the meat retain moisture while cooking.

207. PREVENT DUMPLINGS FROM STICKING

A thin layer of olive oil in the steamer basket will prevent dumplings from sticking.

208. GET CRISPY SALMON SKIN

A skin-on whole fish will be crispier if you rub the outside of the fish's skin with olive oil. Wash and pat dry first.

209. CRISP POULTRY SKIN

After washing and patting dry, rub EVOO over the skin of poultry and it will crisp up nicely in the oven.

210. KEEP COOKED PASTA FROM CLUMPING

As soon as pasta is done, pour it into a colander and let it drain, then lightly toss with a small quantity of good-quality EVOO.

211. MAKE IT LAST

Store olive oil in a cool, dark place to make it last longer. If it came in a clear glass bottle, consider decanting it into something darker that won't let light in. Both light and heat will cause it to deteriorate.

DRIZZLE IT

Extra virgin olive oil makes a wonderful condiment. Drizzle it on almost any food to enhance its flavor. Add a dash of sea salt and fresh black pepper to finish.

212. Drizzle over fresh mozzarella.

213. Drizzle over sliced tomatoes.

214. Drizzle over a baked potato instead of using butter.

215. Drizzle over toasted slices of crusty bread.

216. Drizzle over popcorn.

217. Drizzle over steamed vegetables.

218. Drizzle over pizza.

219. Drizzle over white beans.

220. Drizzle over fried or scrambled eggs.

221. Drizzle over grilled portabella mushrooms.

222. Drizzle it on vanilla ice cream.

223. Drizzle it on HEARTY soupS.

224. Drizzle it over sautéed shrimp.

225. Drizzle it over corn-on-the-cob instead of butter.

226. Drizzle it over freshly grilled fish.

227. Drizzle it over toasted nuts.

228. Drizzle it over sweet potato fries.

229. KEEP BASIL PESTO GREEN

Pour a thin layer of EVOO over your pesto before sealing in a container to keep it green. The oil sits on top of the blend and prevents the top layer from oxidizing.

230. INFUSE IT WITH GARLIC

Easy and delicious, garlic-infused olive oil is wonderful for dipping a fresh baguette or drizzling over vegetables. Fill a sterilized, dry bottle with EVOO. Drop in one clove of garlic; let stand for several days. Use within a week.

231. INFUSE IT—SAFELY

Homemade infused oils are a delight and make wonderful gifts. However, it is important to know that even a trace of water or moisture can cause bacterial growth in your oil, even in a sealed bottle. Any herb or ingredient you plan to use in your infused oil must be dried completely before use.

ALWAYS STORE INFUSED OILS IN THE REFRIGATOR AND USE WITHIN ONE WEEK OF MAKING THEM.

232. POUR OVER PASTA

A full-flavored EVOO and some salt and pepper are all you need for a simple pasta sauce.

233. PREVENT BUTTER FROM BURNING

A few drops of olive oil in the pan will prevent butter from burning.

234. BAKE HEALTHY

In baking, substitute ⅓ cup (80 mL) olive oil for each stick of butter. Choose a light-tasting olive oil for baking. The results will be delicious and have less fat and fewer calories.

235. WHIP IT

For healthier mashed potatoes, substitute olive oil for butter and whip the ingredients together for a fluffy, tasty result.

236. MAKE BAKED POTATO CHIPS

Slice potatoes thinly and coat with olive oil and sea salt, then spread flat on a baking sheet and bake at 400°F (200°C) until they reach desired crispness.

237. LUBRICATE GRILL RACKS

Brush clean racks with olive oil before turning on the grill to prevent food from sticking.

238. GREASE BAKING DISHES

A healthier way to grease a pan is to use olive oil instead of butter.

239. HOLD THE MAYO

EVOO makes a great mayo replacement in sandwiches. Drizzle a bit over your bread just as you would have spread the mayo.

MARINATE BEFORE GRILLING

Combining the rich flavor of olive oil with an acid such as vinegar or lemon juice, and your choice of herbs and spices will yield any number of flavor-enhancing marinades for meat, fish, poultry, and vegetables. Marinating makes food moist and more flavorful, particularly if you are grilling. Simply coat the meat, fish, or vegetables lightly and evenly in a shallow baking dish or even a plastic bag, and let sit for 20 minutes to several hours. For safety, if you are marinating longer than an hour, do it in the refrigerator.

240. FRESH FISH MARINADE
3 tablespoons (45 mL) olive oil
3 tablespoons (45 mL) white wine
3 tablespoons (45 mL) fresh lemon juice
Sea salt and black pepper to taste

241. CHICKEN BREAST MARINADE
1 tablespoon (15 mL) red wine vinegar
2 teaspoons (10 mL) dried rosemary
1 tablespoon (15 mL) Dijon-style mustard
1 teaspoon (5 mL) garlic, minced
¼ cup (120 mL) extra virgin olive oil
Sea salt and black pepper to taste

242. VEGGIE MARINADE

½ cup (120 mL) extra virgin olive oil
½ cup (120 mL) lemon juice
½ cup (120 mL) soy sauce
1 clove fresh garlic, minced

243. ROSEMARY MARINADE FOR PORK

2 tablespoons (30 mL) fresh rosemary, chopped
2 tablespoons (30 mL) fresh garlic, minced
3 tablespoons (45 mL) lemon juice
¼ cup (60 mL) extra virgin olive oil
sea salt and black pepper to taste

244. ULTIMATE MARINADE
FOR FISH, MEAT, OR VEGETABLES

¼ cup (60 mL) lemon juice
½ teaspoon (3 mL) black pepper
½ teaspoon (3 mL) sea salt
2 tablespoons (30 mL) lemon zest
½ cup (120 mL) extra virgin olive oil
3 cloves garlic, minced
¼ cup (60 mL) fresh parsley, chopped
¼ cup (60 mL) fresh basil or oregano, chopped

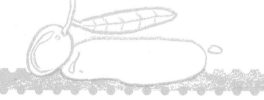

245. PREVENT WATER FROM BOILING OVER

Add a teaspoon of olive oil to the pot of water to prevent it from boiling over and making a mess of your stovetop.

246. TRY A TRADITIONAL STEAK FLORENTINE

For this Tuscan recipe, you'll need a nice T-bone. Pat down both sides liberally with sea salt and grill to desired doneness, then remove from heat, drizzle with olive oil, and serve.

247. ENHANCE HUMMUS

Drizzle over store-bought hummus to add more flavor—and sprinkle with freshly chopped parsley as a garnish.

248. DE-STAIN MUGS

Coffee, tea, and other stains inside mugs will respond to a good scrubbing with baking soda on a wet sponge or scrubber.

249. MAKE YOUR OWN BAKING POWDER

- 1 teaspoon (5 mL) baking soda
- 2 teaspoons (10 mL) cream of tartar
- 1 teaspoon (5 mL) corn starch (optional)

When a recipe calls for baking powder but you've run out, whip up a batch of your own using baking soda. Use immediately.

250. CLEAN UP THE MICROWAVE

A paste of baking soda and water, applied with a clean sponge or cloth, is great for restoring a dirty microwave oven to pristine cleanliness.

251. SCOUR OFF CRUSTED-ON FOOD

Sprinkle a generous amount of baking soda into a seriously dirty pot or pan, then add warm water and a squeeze of dishwashing liquid. Let sit for 10 minutes. Work at dirty spots with a sponge or scrubber. Wash as usual.

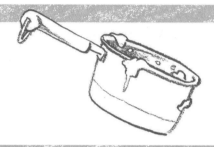

252. SIMMER A DIRTY POT

- ¼ cup (60 mL) baking soda

Pots with cooked-on food may be restored to cleanliness with a solution of baking soda. Pour into the pot and fill with water. Bring to a boil, then lower heat and simmer for 10 minutes. Remove from heat and let stand for 45 minutes. Pour out the water, scrape down the sides, and wash as usual.

253. KEEP LEMONS AT ROOM TEMPERATURE

Lemons kept at room temperature will yield more juice than cold lemons.

254. GET MORE JUICE FROM YOUR LEMON

Before juicing, roll a lemon firmly between your hand and the kitchen counter or other hard surface.

255. IMPROVE THE TASTE OF WATER

If your local tap water is safe but not delicious, a few drops of lemon juice will make it much more palatable.

256. PERK UP A COLA

Serve cola with a slim wedge of lemon.

257. PREVENT RICE
FROM CLUMPING

Add a teaspoon (5 mL) of lemon juice to the water when boiling rice.

258. SQUEEZE
IT OVER STEAK

A few squeezes of fresh lemon over a grilled steak is a wonderful way to liven up an old staple.

259. PREVENT CUT
APPLES FROM BROWNING

To keep cut apples from turning brown, spritz them with lemon juice or put them in a bath of lemon juice and water.

260. KEEP
GUACAMOLE GREEN

Lemon juice can prevent avocados from browning; add it to guacamole to keep the color bright.

261. KEEP CUT POTATOES
FROM DISCOLORING

As with apples, potatoes, which are also white-fleshed, will not brown if you keep them in cold water with a splash of lemon juice.

262. REVIVE
WILTED LETTUCE

To bring drooping lettuce back from the brink, fill the (clean) sink with cold water and squeeze in the juice of one lemon. Let the greens sit in the water for a full hour, then spin dry.

263. GARNISH
A GLASS OF WATER

A wedge of lemon makes a plain glass of water look more appealing, and many people enjoy the fresh scent and flavor in their drink. A half slice or a wedge will do the trick.

264. "COOK" FISH WITH
LEMON JUICE

The Latin American tradition of "cooking" seafood in citrus is easy, healthy, and goes back to Incan times, when the ancient peoples of South America preserved fish with lemon juice. You can do it, too—simply marinate almost any fish or shellfish in lemon juice.

265. SUBSTITUTE
GREMOLATA FOR SALT

This Italian condiment can be used to brighten up almost any dish, and is especially useful if you are watching your salt intake. Mix equal parts lemon zest, minced garlic, and chopped fresh parsley.

266. MAKE LEMON SIMPLE SYRUP

- Zest of one lemon
- ¾ cup (175 mL) fresh lemon juice
- 2 cups (500 mL) sugar
- 2 cups (500 mL) water

Lemon simple syrup is good to have on hand for baking and for adding flavor to drinks such as iced tea or carbonated water. Heat zest, sugar, and water in a small saucepan, stirring until sugar dissolves. Bring to a boil, then remove from heat. Sieve and discard solids. Stir in lemon juice. Store in refrigerator for up to 4 weeks.

267. ADD A TWIST TO A COCKTAIL

A perfect spiral of lemon adds flair to any cocktail, while the oils in the peel flavor the drink itself. To do it, you need a very sharp paring knife or vegetable peeler. Wash the lemon thoroughly and dry it. Carefully cut a strip about a ½-inch (1.2 cm) wide and 3 inches (7.5 cm) long. Cut off the ends neatly. Wrap the strip around a metal skewer in a spiral then slide off onto the edge of the drink.

268. MAKE HOMEMADE LEMONADE

- ½ cup (120 mL) sugar
- ½ cup (120 mL) water
- 6 lemons, juiced

Combine water and sugar, bring to a boil, stir until sugar is dissolved. Let cool. In a pitcher, combine syrup with lemon juice and stir.

269. MAKE CEVICHE

- 2 pounds (1 kg) firm white fish
- juice of 8 to 12 lemons, strained
- 1 red onion, minced
- 2 teaspoons (10 mL) fresh cilantro, chopped
- 1 teaspoon (5 mL) salt
- pepper to taste

Place fish in a nonreactive baking dish. Mix ingredients together and pour over fish to cover. Let marinate in refrigerator for 2–3 hours. Serve.

270. CANDY LEMON PEELS

- 2 to 4 lemons
- 1 cup (250 mL) sugar plus more for sprinkling
- 1 cup (250 mL) water

With a sharp paring knife, cut off peel, leaving some pith on. Slice into strips about a ¼ inch (6 mm) wide. Cook peels in boiling water for about 8 to 10 minutes or until tender. Place cooked peels on a wire rack to cool for 12 minutes. In a small saucepan, bring 1 cup (250 mL) of water to a boil and dissolve 1 cup (250 mL) sugar. Drop peels into boiling water and cook about 10 minutes or until peels are translucent. Remove peels to drying rack and let cool completely. Coat with sugar. Great for garnishes!

271. ENJOY A LEMON SLUSH

- juice of ½ lemon
- ice cubes
- sugar to taste

Mix the lemon juice and ice cubes in the blender until you achieve slushy consistency; add sugar to taste. Pour into a cup and enjoy the lemon chill.

MAKE (ALMOST)
ANY FOOD ZESTIER

Lemon zest adds an intense and satisfying burst of flavor without extra liquid or calories. It improves everything from sauces to pie crusts. A microplane grater (or your preferred other zesting tool) is a kitchen essential that makes it easy to quickly and efficiently add fresh lemon zest to any dish. You can also dry grated zest and keep it on hand to brighten the flavor of almost anything.

Experiment with adding zest in differing amounts. A tiny pinch or a light dusting can add just a hint of brightness, while a more generous spoonful will infuse the entire dish with lemony goodness.

272. Add zest to cookie dough.

273. Add zest to pie crust.

274. Add zest to cake flour.

275. Add zest to muffin mix.

276. Add zest to pancakes.

277. Add zest to rice dishes.

278. Add zest to tomato sauce.

279. Add zest to home-brewed beer.

280. Add zest to pasta dishes.

281. Add zest to grain dishes.

282. Add zest to bean dishes.

283. Add zest to potato dishes.

284. Add zest to salads or dressings.

285. Add zest to homemade jams.

286. Add zest to tea (hot or iced)

287. Add zest to whipped cream.

288. Add zest to breadcrumbs.

289. Garnish soups with zest.

290. Sprinkle zest over steamed or roasted vegetables.

291. Add zest to ice cubes.

292. Add zest to fish.

293. Add zest to marinades.

294. Add zest to sauces.

295. PRESERVE LEMONS

- 7 or 8 Meyer lemons, scrubbed clean and dried
- ½ cup (120 mL) salt
- sterile canning jar

Pour 1 teaspoon (5 mL) salt into the bottom of the jar. Cut the lemons so they are almost quartered but still connected at the bottom. Gently push them open and sprinkle salt all over the lemon flesh. Close them up again, and place them in the jar, squishing them down so the juice fills up the jar. Add more freshly squeezed if necessary, then top with more salt. Seal jar and let sit at room temperature or in the refrigerator for 30 days, regularly turning the jar. When ready to use, rinse off the salt. Store in the refrigerator up to 6 months.

296. MAKE TANGY ICE CUBES

A drop of lemon juice in each ice cube compartment is all you need.

297. LIVEN UP TUNA SALAD

Squeeze a slim wedge of lemon juice over tuna fish salad to give it a fresher taste.

298. MAKE LEMON CURD

- ½ cup (120 mL) freshly squeezed lemon juice, strained
- 2 teaspoons (10 mL) fresh lemon zest, finely grated
- ½ cup (120 mL) sugar
- 3 large eggs
- 6 tablespoons (¾ stick) unsalted butter, cut into bits

Cream together butter and sugar; whisk in eggs, then juice and zest, until smooth. (It will look curdled.) Pour into a double boiler and cook over moderate heat, stirring frequently, until curd is thick and temperature is 170°F (77°C). Do not allow mixture to boil. Transfer lemon curd to a bowl, cover surface tightly with plastic wrap, then refrigerate at least 1 hour. Store in refrigerator up to a week.

CHAPTER 3
Health, Hygiene, And Beauty

A NOTE ON SAFETY

Although the tips in this book have been carefully researched, they are not a substitute for professional advice. Before using any of the suggestions in this book, please see a doctor to make sure that you make healthy decisions.

299. EXFOLIATE YOUR BODY

- 1 cup (250 mL) sea salt
- ½ cup (120 mL) olive oil

A salt scrub makes an invigorating all-over exfoliator and an excellent spot softener for callused areas such as the feet. The coarse grains of sea salt are perfect. Mix ingredients together in a bowl and apply with hands or a washcloth, rubbing gently. Add herbs such as rosemary or lemon rind for a more aromatic experience.

300. GENTLY CLEAN OILY SKIN

- ½ teaspoon (3 mL) sea salt
- 2 tablespoons (30 mL) plain yogurt
- 1 egg white

Mix the salt and yogurt in a small bowl. In a separate bowl, whisk the egg white until frothy. Combine the two. Apply to face with fingertips, gently massaging in a circular motion. Rinse thoroughly and pat dry.

301. BATHE BRUISES

- 2 cups (500 mL) Epsom salt

Pour Epsom salts under running water into bathtub until dissolved. Soak the bruise for 15 minutes.

302. DE-PUFF EYES

Soak cotton balls in salt water and place them on puffy eyelids for 5 minutes. If you chill them in the refrigerator for a few minutes, you'll boost their ability to take down the swollen tissues.

303. RELAX WITH SEA SALT AND LAVENDER

- 2 tablespoons sea salt
- 6 drops lavender essential oil

Soak your stress away in a relaxing, aromatic bath. Turn on the faucet and adjust the temperature so it is nicely warm but not too hot, then add a couple of heaping teaspoons of sea salt under the flow. When the tub is full, pour in the 6 drops of lavender essential oil and swish. Now enjoy a spa-like experience in your own home!

304. GET WAVY HAIR

- 1 tablespoon (15 mL) sea salt
- teaspoon (5 mL) lemon juice
- 3 cups (750 mL) hot water

Combine ingredients in a spray bottle. Spray on hair and scrunch to create "beachy" waves.

305. EASE AN EARACHE

Fill an old sock with salt and warm it in the microwave for about 10 to 15 seconds. TEST to make sure it is warm, but not hot. Lay the warm sock against the affected ear to soothe it.

306. EASE TIRED FEET

- ½ cup (120 mL) Epsom salt or sea salt
- warm water

Try this simple callus-softening, odor-eliminating bath for tired feet. A 10-minute soak will leave your aching feet feeling much better, softer, and sweeter-smelling.

307. GET THE ITCH OUT

Soothe the site of an itchy insect bite or sting with a paste of salt. Either table salt or sea salt will do. Mix enough salt with water to make a paste that will cover the affected area. Let dry and brush off.

308. SOOTHE A SUNBURN

- 2 tablespoons (30 mL) Epsom salt
- 1 cup (250 mL) water

Combine salt and water in a bowl. Soak a washcloth in the saltwater and lay over irritated skin for 10 minutes.

309. ADD VOLUME TO THIN HAIR

Combine equal parts Epsom salt and your regular volumizing conditioner. Work mixture through hair; leave in for 10 minutes then rinse and style as usual.

310. ALLEVIATE MUSCLE SORENESS

A heavier-than-usual workout may leave you sore all over. Pour 2 cups (500 mL) of Epsom salt under the running faucet as you fill a warm tub. Relax and soak for at least 15 minutes.

311. MAKE YOUR OWN ISOTONIC SALINE SOLUTION

- 2 teaspoons (10 mL) non-iodized salt
- 4 cups (1 mL) water

A saline solution that is approximately the same concentration as human tears is called isotonic, or normal, saline solution. It is useful for gargling, using as a mouthwash, and rinsing scrapes or minor wounds, among other home remedies. Pour the water into a clean pot, add the salt, and boil with the lid on for 15 minutes. Allow to cool to room temperature before removing the lid and pouring into a sterile container. Use within 24 hours.

312. MAKE A HYPERTONIC SALINE SOLUTION

- 1 teaspoon (5 mL) non-iodized salt
- 1 cup (250 mL) water

A hypertonic solution is one that is saltier than your body's tissues. It is primariy useful for irrigating extremely congested nasal tissues.

313. REMOVE
TEMPORARY TATTOOS

A handful of salt rubbed on the remains of a temporary tattoo will erase those last bits still clinging to skin.

314. TREAT A
FLAKY SCALP

A natural dandruff treatment to get rid of flakes consists of a gentle, three-minute scalp massage with a handful of salt before shampooing as usual with anti-dandruff shampoo. The salt will help remove any flakes that have accumulated on your scalp.

315. COMFORT A CANKER

- 1 teaspoon (5 mL) salt
- 8 ounces (120 mL) warm water

Alleviate the pain of these annoying sores by rinsing with salt water. Swish around the mouth for one minute. Repeat as needed.

316. SOOTHE A SORE THROAT

- 1 teaspoon (5 mL) salt
- 1 cup (250 mL) warm water

Gargling with saltwater is a time-tested home remedy to ease a sore throat due to cold. Stir the salt into a cup of warm water and gargle for one minute.

317. IRRIGATE THE EYES

- ½ teaspoon non-iodized salt
- 8 ounces sterile distilled water

For conjunctivitis, always consult a doctor. A natural treatment that can you can try in addition to following your doctor's orders is to irrigate the affected eye with a sterile salt water solution. You can purchase distilled water at the pharmacy or make your own by boiling it for 15 minutes. Let it stand until cool, and pour into a sterile jar.

318. SOFTEN SKIN

- 1 cup (250 mL) sea salt

Slowly pour a cup of sea salt under the running water as you fill your bath, then soak for 10 minutes to soften skin all over.

319. MAKE YOUR OWN MOUTHWASH

Equal parts salt and baking soda dissolved in water makes an effective homemade mouthwash that fights odor-causing bacteria. Swish for one minute and spit.

320. LENGTHEN THE LIFE OF YOUR TOOTHBRUSH

Soak your toothbrush in a saline solution for 60 minutes to eliminate bacteria that build up after regular use. This will help your brush last longer.

321. TRY HALOTHERAPY FOR CONGESTION

Although clinical research is as yet in short supply, traditional practitioners have long suggested salt therapy, or halotherapy, for nasal and lung congestion. They believe that inhaling salt mist will ease congested passages. There are several ways to try out the benefits of halotherapy: visit a salt cave or mine such as Wieliska in Poland; try a commercial salt spa with a salt "cave" that has been constructed for this purpose and into which salt mist is usually blown; or test out a halogenerator, a device that aerosolizes salt for home use.

322. OPEN CONGESTED NASAL PASSAGES

An isotonic or hypertonic saline solution is a proven tool in the battle against a stuffy nose. You can use a neti pot or purchase a nasal irrigation device for this purpose. Irrigate one nostril and allow the solution to drain out of the other nostril, then repeat on the other side.

323. SMOOTH SKIN

- 1 cup (250 mL) white vinegar
- ½ cup (120 mL) baking soda
- ½ cup (120 mL) uncooked oatmeal

Pour ingredients into hot bathwater. Enjoy a long soak and emerge with your skin feeling renewed.

324. CLEAN AND TONE YOUR SKIN

Soak a cotton ball in white vinegar and gently skim over your face and neck to pick up dirt and tighten pores.

325. APPLY AFTERSHAVE

A natural astringent, apple cider vinegar makes an excellent aftershave. Mix equal parts apple cider vinegar and water, and splash on skin after shaving.

326. TIGHTEN AND TONE

- 2 tablespoons (30 mL) apple cider vinegar
- 2 tablespoons fresh mint leaves, crushed
- 1 cup (250 mL) purified or distilled water

Place mint in a sterilized glass jar, add water and vinegar. Shake well. Let sit for 3 days, then strain into a clean container. Apply to skin with a cotton ball for a refreshing toner.

327. GET SHINIER HAIR

- 1 tablespoon (15 mL) white or apple cider vinegar
- 1 cup (250 mL) water

Shampoo, conditioner, and styling products can leave residues that dull your hair. A vinegar rinse is a natural way to dissolve these residues. Mix the vinegar into the water and use to rinse freshly shampooed hair. Rinse again with plain water. Dry as usual.

328. MOISTURIZE
WITH A MASK

- ½ teaspoon (3 mL) apple cider vinegar
- 1 teaspoon (5 mL) honey
- 1 egg, separated

Blend vinegar, honey, and egg yolk. Beat egg white until frothy and mix with vinegar mixture. Apply to face. Leave on 10 minutes then rinse.

329. CLEAN
GRUBBY HANDS

- 1 tablespoon (15 mL) apple cider vinegar
- 1 tablespoon (15 mL) cornmeal

Combine to make a paste that will get even the dirtiest hands clean—and they'll feel softer, too.

330. RELIEVE
SORE MUSCLES

- 3 cups (750 ml) apple cider vinegar

Pour the vinegar into a hot bath and soak for 30 minutes to relieve aching muscles from overwork or strenuous exercise.

331. SOFTEN FEET

- 1 teaspoon (5 mL) white vinegar
- 1 tablespoon (15 mL) olive oil
- 1 teaspoon (5 mL) honey (optional)

Mix into a paste and massage into feet. Put on a pair of cotton socks, and leave them on overnight. In the morning, scrub feet clean with a washcloth and dry thoroughly.

332. SOFTEN CALLUSED HEELS

- 1 tablespoon (15 mL) rice vinegar
- 1 tablespoon (15 mL) honey
- 1 tablespoon (15 mL) coarse salt

Make a paste and use to scrub heels and other tough areas of feet.

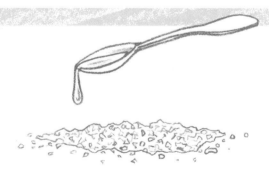

333. CLEAN
HAIR IMPLEMENTS

- 3 tablespoons (45 mL) white vinegar
- 3 tablespoons (45 mL) baking soda
- bowl of warm water

Freshen up your combs and brushes with this trick: sprinkle baking soda over them, then pour on the vinegar, and let fizz for a few minutes. Then soak the combs and brushes in warm water for an hour or two. Dry completely.

334. MAKE NAIL
POLISH LAST

Before applying polish, dip nails into a solution of equal parts white vinegar and water; let them soak for one minute, then rinse and dry thoroughly.

335. WARD OFF WARTS

A minor wart can be treated with this home remedy: apply full-strength apple cider vinegar to a cotton ball. Tape the cotton ball onto the wart with a bandage or first-aid tape, and leave it on overnight. In the morning, remove and wash with soap and water; allow to dry completely. Repeat for 10 days.

336. TRY AN OLD-FASHIONED ARTHRITIS TONIC

A recipe passed down for generations calls for drinking a cup (250 mL) daily of the following mixture: 5 parts grape juice, 3 parts honey, and 1 part raw, unfiltered apple cider vinegar.

337. FIGHT FOOT FUNGUS

If your foot odor is the result of fungus (such as athlete's foot), a stronger vinegar solution will help. Pour equal parts apple cider vinegar and warm water into a foot bath; soak the affected feet for 15 minutes morning and night.

338. TREAT A SUNBURN

White vinegar can take out some of the sting from too much time spent in the sun. Pour it into a spray bottle, refrigerate until cold, then spray on the affected skin.

339. EASE SWOLLEN JOINTS

- 1 cup (250 mL) apple cider vinegar
- 1 cup (250 mL) water

In a saucepan or microwave, warm the vinegar and water. Wet a clean cloth with the mixure and apply to aching joints. Let sit for 5 minutes.

340. EXTRACT A SPLINTER

Soak the afflicted area in full-strength white vinegar for 30 minutes to help draw the splinter to the surface for removal.

341. ATTACK ACNE

A toner of equal parts apple cider vinegar and water, applied with a cotton ball to areas of your face or body that are prone to acne, may help to prevent breakouts.

342. SOOTHE A RASH

The itching that accompanies mild rashes such as that caused by heat, poison ivy, or contact dermatitis, may be eased by dabbing on apple cider vinegar. Moisten a soft cloth with the vinegar. Try putting it in the refrigerator for an hour first so the cloth is nice and cool.

343. DISCOURAGE KIDNEY STONES

- 1 teaspoon (5 mL) apple cider vinegar
- 6 ounces (175 mL) water

This old folk remedy calls for mixing the vinegar into the water and drinking one glass daily.

344. GET RID OF GAS

- 1 teaspoon (5 mL) raw, unfiltered apple cider vinegar
- 1 teaspoon (5 mL) honey
- 1 cup (250 mL) water

Mix vinegar and honey into the water, and drink it to ease the discomfort and bloating of gas.

345. DECONTAMINATE SOCKS

Soak smelly socks (particularly if you are subject to fungal conditions) in a mixture of 1 part white vinegar to 4 parts water for an hour before laundering in hot water.

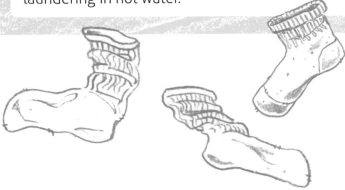

346. WHITEN DISCOLORED TOENAILS

- 5 tablespoons (75 mL) white vinegar
- 1 cup (250 mL) water

Regularly wearing polish can cause yellowing of the toenails. Combine vinegar and water in a footbath or large bowl and soak your toes for 30 minutes to lighten the discoloration. Rinse and moisturize.

347. SOOTHE HEMORRHOIDS

Cotton balls soaked in full-strength white vinegar and chilled in the refrigerator may provide relief from the pain of piles.

348. DESENSITIZE MOSQUITO BITES

If you know you've gotten a mosquito bite and you've not yet scratched, you can reduce the itch factor by dabbing it with full-strength white vinegar.

349. DETER URINARY TRACT INFECTIONS

- 2 tablespoons (30 mL) apple cider vinegar
- 1 teaspoon (5 mL) honey
- 1 cup (250 mL) water

Mix ingredients completely, drink one glass daily.

350. CLEAR COLD CONGESTION

- 1 teaspoon (5 mL) raw, unfiltered apple cider vinegar
- 1 cup (250 mL) water

A drink of apple cider vinegar mixed in water may thin the mucus that is clogging your nose and throat.

351. CLEAR UP BLEMISHES OVERNIGHT

Mix equal parts white vinegar and water. Dab onto pimples using a cotton swab to dry them out.

352. SOOTHE ITCHY SKIN

- 1 tablespoon (15 mL) apple cider vinegar
- ½ cup (120 mL) tepid water

Mix well. Dip a clean, soft cloth or cotton ball in the mixture and gently dab onto itchy skin.

353. LOSE WEIGHT

- 1 teaspoon (5 mL) raw, unfiltered apple cider vinegar
- 1 cup (250 mL) water

Studies indicate that ingesting vinegar before before meals can help reduce feelings of hunger and increase feelings of satiety—advantageous when you are trying to lose weight! Try a tablespoon (15 mL) of apple cider vinegar in a glass of water and see if it helps you to eat less.

354. SWEETEN STINKY FEET

A generous spritz of full-strength white vinegar onto smelly feet caused by hot shoes will counteract the nasty odor.

355. DISINFECT YOUR TOOTHBRUSH

After suffering from a cold, soak your toothbrush overnight in white vinegar to get rid of germs. Rinse thoroughly before use.

356. COUNTER CANDIDA

- 2 cups (500 mL) white vinegar

A home remedy for yeast infections is to bathe in warm water infused with vinegar. Sit for 10 minutes.

357. PREVENT SWIMMER'S EAR

- 1 part white vinegar
- 1 part rubbing alcohol

To prevent swimmer's ear, use a dropper to pour about 1 teaspoon (5 mL) of this mixture into the ear canal, then tilt head away and let it drain out.

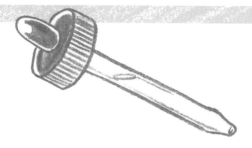

358. STOP HICCUPS

An old-fashioned tactic for ending an attack of hiccups is to down a teaspoon (5 mL) of apple cider vinegar.

359. LOWER CHOLESTEROL

- 2 teaspoons (10 mL) raw, unfiltered apple cider vinegar
- 1 cup (250 mL) apple juice

Some studies have shown that apple cider vinegar may lower cholesterol; if you want to try it, mixing it with juice is a good way to start. Drink one glass daily. Grapefruit juice works, too.

360. COUNTER INDIGESTION

- 1 tablespoon (15 mL) apple cider vinegar
- 1 teaspoon (5 mL) raw honey
- 6 ounces (175 mL) warm water

To calm heartburn, stir together vinegar, honey, and water until combined. Sip.

361. WRAP A SORE THROAT

- 2 tablespoons (30 mL) apple cider vinegar
- 1 cup (250 mL) warm water

Steep a cloth in this mixture. When it is warm but not uncomfortable to the touch, gently squeeze it out and wrap it around your neck and upper chest. Sit in a warm place for an hour or until it cools.

362. TREAT A JELLYFISH STING

The painful aftermath of an encounter with a jellyfish may be eased by splashing full-strength white vinegar over the afflicted skin to deactivate venomous nematocysts, which are responsible for the pain. Follow with hot water, as heat has been shown to deactivate venom.

DO NOT USE VINEGAR FOR PORTUGUESE MAN O' WAR STINGS, SEEK MEDICAL ATTENTION.

363. MOISTURIZE A FLAKY SCALP

Massaging olive oil into the scalp can help loosen flakes and moisturize the scalp to prevent more flaking. Wet hair first. Then apply olive oil directly to the scalp with a cotton ball. Massage vigorously for 3 minutes then let stand for 5 minutes. Wash thoroughly, rinse, and dry.

364. LOOSEN CRADLE CAP

This common, harmless condition causes flaky patches on young babies' scalps. To gently treat cradle cap, you can apply olive oil to baby's scalp with a cotton ball or clean hands. Gently massage into the scalp and leave on for 20 minutes. Use a fine-toothed comb to lift and remove patches, then wash and dry baby's head thoroughly. If cradle cap does not respond to olive oil treatment, ask your pediatrician about an alternative approach.

365. MOISTURIZE DRY SKIN

Since ancient times, olive oil has been considered an ideal body moisturizer, very hydrating and rich in vitamins. Apply it directly to slightly damp skin and allow to sink in.

366. TAKE OFF EYE MAKE-UP

Use olive oil to remove eye make-up, even waterproof products. Saturate a cotton pad or puff with olive oil and use to gently wipe off eye shadow, eyeliner, and mascara.

367. CLEAN MAKE-UP BRUSHES

Keep good quality make-up brushes in top condition by cleaning and conditioning them with olive oil. Work a small amount into the bristles, then wipe gently on a clean paper towel. Rinse thoroughly in warm water and blot dry. Allow to air dry overnight before using.

368. GENTLY EXFOLIATE YOUR FACE

- 1 tablespoon (15 mL) extra virgin olive oil
- 1 teaspoon (5 mL) granulated white sugar

Combine olive oil and sugar in a small bowl. Apply to face with fingertips, using a circular stroke. Massage gently over face, then rinse thoroughly and pat dry.

369. DEEP CONDITION DAMAGED HAIR

- ¼ cup (60 mL) extra virgin olive oil
- ¼ cup (60 mL) hot water

A hot oil treatment does wonders for dry, damaged and dull hair. Combine water and olive oil in a blender until completely emulsified. Test to make sure temperature is not too hot. Pour on hair and comb through. Wrap hair in a towel and let sit for 15 to 30 minutes. Remove towel and wash hair completely—you may need 2 washings to completely remove oil but your hair will be shinier and healthier.

370. RENEW FACIAL
SKIN WITH A MASK

- 1 tablespoon (15 mL) extra virgin olive oil

- 1 egg yolk

- ¼ teaspoon (1 mL) lemon juice

Thoroughly combine ingredients. Apply to clean skin and leave on for 5 minutes, then rinse off.

371. ADD SHINE AND
MOISTURE TO DRY HAIR

- 1 tablespoon (15 mL) honey

- 3 tablespoons (45 mL) olive oil

Heat olive oil and honey in a saucepan on low until combined. Allow to cool slightly until comfortable to the touch. Pour into hair and comb through. Let sit 15 minutes. Wash, condition, and style as usual.

372. CONDITION YOUR PATE

Even if you don't have hair, you can still enjoy the benefits of olive oil on your scalp. Keep a bald pate conditioned with a few drops of olive oil massaged into the skin.

373. TAME FRIZZY HAIR

Just a drop or two of olive oil can replace costly de-frizzing products. Apply a drop to hands, rub it in between palms, and run lightly over hair, paying particular attention to ends.

374. PREVENT WRINKLES

High in vitamin E, olive oil makes an effective anti-aging facial moisturizer and may even help to reduce sun damage. Use your fingertips to apply to clean, damp skin with gentle circular motions.

375. HEAL
CHAPPED LIPS

Olive oil re-hydrates chapped lips beautifully and without chemicals. Simply rub a drop into lips whenever they get dry.

376. MAKE LIP BALM

- 3 tablespoons (45 mL) extra virgin olive oil
- 1 tablespoon (15 mL) beeswax

Heat beeswax and olive oil in a small saucepan, stirring to thoroughly combine. Once melted, remove from heat and allow to cool. Pour into container.

377. SOFTEN HANDS

Rough, dry skin on hands responds quickly to the moisturizing benefits of olive oil.

378. FIX RAGGED CUTICLES

Rub a drop or two of olive oil into dry cuticles to restore them to health.

379. SCRUB YOUR FEET

- 3 cups (750 mL) granulated sugar
- 1 cup (250 mL) olive oil
- essential oil of your choice

Mix ingredients together and store in a glass jar with a lid. Apply liberally to feet and massage. Rinse.

380. MASSAGE SORE MUSCLES

Athletes in ancient Greece are believed to have used olive oil on their skin, and Ayurvedic medicine recommends it for strains and sprains. It makes a good massage oil, particularly for sore muscles. Warm it between the hands first, then apply to skin.

381. TREAT ARTHRITIS

In a study of patients with rheumatoid arthritis, a supplement of approximately 4 tablespoons (60 mL) of extra virgin olive oil taken daily was found to reduce pain and stiffness. You can add it to your food or take it directly—but if you decide to try it, be sure to replace other fats in your diet with the olive oil, rather than simply to add it on top of what you are already consuming.

382. GET A SMOOTH SHAVE

Unlike most commercial shaving creams and gels, olive oil lubricates and hydrates the skin, giving a closer, better shave and leaving skin soft and rejuvenated. Ideal for sensitive skin, olive oil is perfect for shaving the face, legs, and underarms.

383. REMOVE GUM FROM HAIR

Work several drops of olive oil into the gum and surrounding hair and wait 3 minutes. Use fingers or a comb to remove the gum.

384. LOWER CHOLESTEROL

The monounsaturated fatty acids in extra virgin olive oil may help to inhibit the damaging effects of LDL or "bad" cholesterol. The key is to replace other fats in your diet with olive oil; about 2 tablespoons (30 mL) per day is optimal.

385. LOOSEN EAR WAX

Soften a build-up of ear wax with a couple drops of olive oil a day. Lie on one side, and use a clean dropper to insert warm (body temperature) olive oil into the ear. Stay still for several minutes. Repeat on the other side. When you stand up, be sure to hold a washcloth to your ear to catch any drips. Repeat daily for up to 10 days to soften ear wax.

386. REMOVE PAINT FROM HAIR AND SKIN

Drips of paint that ended up on your hair and skin can be removed with olive oil. Saturate a cotton ball and run it over the paint that is stuck to you until the paint loosens. Wipe it off, then wash with soap and rinse.

387. SMOTHER LICE

As parents of small children know, lice treatment is a multi-stage process that requires not just killing the critters but removing the nits. Olive oil is a non-toxic substance for smothering live lice on your child's head. Saturate the child's scalp and hair with olive oil, and place a shower cap over the child's head—let sit for several hours or overnight (you may want to cover the pillow with a towel). You'll need to follow with a thorough comb-out using a fine-toothed lice/nits comb.

388. HELP COMB
OUT NITS

To make tiny nits easier to comb out, add a hefty sprinkle of baking soda to whatever smothering substance (olive oil or conditioner) you have used to saturate the scalp and hair.

389. MAKE YOUR OWN
TOOTHPASTE

Baking soda is a common ingredient in commercial toothpastes, but why not make your own? Simply mix 1 part salt to 2 parts baking soda to form a paste, and apply it to your toothbrush as usual.

390. FRESHEN
UP A RETAINER

• 2 teaspoons (10 mL) baking soda

Dissolve the baking soda in warm water. Place the retainer (or any other oral apparatus) in the water and let it soak off food particles and other residue. Take it out after 15 minutes and rinse.

391. SOOTHE CANKER SORES

- ½ teaspoon (3 mL) baking soda
- 4 ounces (120 mL) warm water

Make a soothing mouth rinse to take the sting out of canker sores on the gums. Dissolve the baking soda completely in a small glass of warm water, and swish in the mouth for 30 seconds.

392. MAKE A MILD FACIAL CLEANSING MILK

- 1 tablespoon (15 mL) baking soda
- 2 tablespoons (30 mL) water
- ¼ cup (60 mL) milk

Thoroughly combine ingredients. Use a soft washcloth to apply to face with gentle circular motions, then rinse off. Pat dry.

393. EXFOLIATE YOUR FACE

- ½ teaspoon (3 mL) baking soda
- handful of facial cleanser

Bring exfoliating action to your facial cleanser by adding a small amount of baking soda. Apply to the face with gentle, circular motions, then rinse off completely, and follow with moisturizer for super-soft skin.

394. RELIEVE BUG BITES AND STINGS

A paste of equal parts baking soda and water can be daubed onto the site of any bite or sting to ease the pain and itch. Let it dry, and don't brush it off.

395. SOAK SORE FEET

- ½ teaspoon (3 mL) baking soda
- 2 quarts (2 L) warm water

Plunge your aching tootsies into a refreshing footbath of baking soda dissolved into warm water. Enjoy the soak for 10 minutes, then dry off.

396. SOOTHE HEARTBURN

- ½ teaspoon (3 mL) baking soda

- 4 ounces (120 ml) water

If you are not on a sodium-restricted diet, you may be able to use baking soda to ease simple heartburn or acid indigestion. Check with your doctor first. Measure carefully, then stir the baking soda into the water until it fully dissolves. Drink one glass every two hours and do not exceed more than 3 doses in 24 hours. If heartburn continues, see your doctor.

397. SOOTHE DIAPER RASH

- 3 tablespoons (45 mL) baking soda

Ease the discomfort of diaper rash with a baking soda bath. Sprinkle the baking soda into warm water in the bottom of a baby tub and let baby sit for a few moments. Be sure to dry baby's bottom thoroughly and apply soothing diaper cream.

398. ENHANCE
YOUR SHAMPOO

- ½ teaspoon (3 mL) baking soda

Give your favorite shampoo a cleaning boost with a handful of baking soda. Pour your usual amount of shampoo into your hand, mix in the baking soda and shampoo as usual. Your hair will be cleaner than ever.

399. FEND OFF
FOOT ODOR

- ½ cup (120 mL) baking soda
- 5 drops lavender or peppermint essential oil
- 2 quarts (2 L) warm water

Dissolve the ingredients in a footbath. Soak your feet in it for at least 10 minutes, then completely dry feet.

400. FIGHT DANDRUFF

In the shower, wet your hair and scalp thoroughly, then sprinkle a few shakes of baking soda onto your head. Massage gently into your scalp then rinse out entirely. Do this regularly to combat dandruff.

401. USE A NATURAL DEODORANT

On days when you don't need full-strength protection, dust baking soda under your arms for a non-chemical deodorant.

402. FIGHT ACNE

A mask of baking soda can dry oily, acne-prone skin. Mix baking soda into warm water to make a light paste. Smooth over skin. Let sit 3 minutes and rinse thoroughly. Pat dry. Use once a week.

403. REMOVE A SPLINTER

Make a paste of baking soda and water, and apply to the area where the splinter is stuck. Place a bandage over it and let sit overnight. It will soften the skin around the splinter and help draw it to the surface for easier removal.

404. TAKE A REFRESHING BATH

- ½ cup (120 mL) baking soda

Stir a handful of baking soda into your bathwater for a more refreshing experience. Added bonus: it deodorizes and softens skin.

405. SOAK AWAY ITCHING

- ½ cup (120 mL) baking soda
- warm water

Soothe itchy skin by bathing in baking soda. Pour it under warm, not hot, running water, then sit in the tub for 10 minutes. Pat dry and moisturize.

406. SCRUB
DIRTY HANDS

For extra-dirty hands, add a handful of baking soda to your cleanser and let the abrasive action of the baking soda work off the dirt. Your hands will be clean and soft.

407. DRY SHAMPOO
YOUR HAIR

When you need a quick hair refresher but there is no opportunity for a full shampoo, a sprinkle of baking soda can be applied to your scalp. Lightly massage and then vigorously brush out.

408. SOFTEN ELBOWS

- ½ teaspoon (3 mL) baking soda
- ½ teaspoon (3 mL) lemon juice

Mix into a paste and apply to rough skin of elbows (or elsewhere). Let sit 5 minutes and rinse off.

409. ENJOY A FIZZY LEMON-SCENTED BATH

- 1 tablespoon (15 mL) baking soda
- 1 tablespoon (15 mL) sea salt
- 1 tablespoon (15 mL) lemon juice

Mix thoroughly in a bowl or jar. Add to running water and enjoy a fizzy bath.

410. TAKE A RELAXING BATH

- 4 tablespoons (60 mL) baking soda
- 1 cup (250 mL) honey
- 2 cups (500 mL) milk

Combine ingredients in a bowl. Swish into bath water for a relaxing, moisturizing experience.

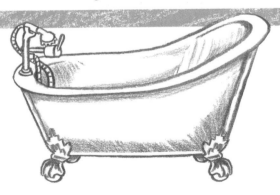

411. KEEP YOUR SYSTEM MOVING

1 teaspoon (5 mL) lemon juice

1 teaspoon (5 mL) honey

1 cup (250 mL) warm water

A gentle way to keep your digestion moving is to drink a glass of this lemon-honey water every morning.

412. LIGHTEN HAIR

• Juice of 3 to 4 lemons

Strain and apply directly to strands of hair you want to lighten. Blow dry or sit in the sun for an hour (use sunscreen on your skin). Then wash and style as usual.

413. RELIEVE A
SORE THROAT

- 1 teaspoon (5 mL) honey
- 2 teaspoon (10 mL) lemon juice

Mix and swallow.

414. LIGHTEN
DARK SPOTS ON SKIN

- ½ lemon
- ½ teaspoon sugar

To lighten freckles or spots on hands, sprinkle sugar on cut side of lemon and dab on spots; don't use on face.

415. BANISH
BAD BREATH

- Juice of 1 lemon
- ¼ cup (60 mL) cool water

Strain the juice and mix it into the water, then swish in the mouth for one minute.

416. DISCOURAGE DANDRUFF

- ½ cup (120 mL) lemon juice
- 1 cup (250 mL) warm water

Mix and apply to freshly washed hair and scalp: leave on for 5 minutes then rinse thoroughly.

417. SOOTHE A COLD

- 1 teaspoon (5 mL) honey
- 2 teaspoon (10 mL) lemon juice
- 1 cup (250 mL) hot water

This soothing sip will ease the sore throat and congestion associated with a cold.

418. TONE OILY SKIN

- 1 teaspoon (5 mL) witch hazel
- 1 teaspoon (5 mL) lemon juice
- 2 tablespoons (30 mL) water

Combine ingredients in a bowl and dip a cotton ball into the mixture. Use it to skim the surface of face and décolletage.

419. WHITEN TEETH

- ½ teaspoon (3 mL) lemon juice
- ½ teaspoon (3 mL) salt
- 1 cup (250 mL) warm water

Dissolve salt into water, add lemon juice. Swish in mouth for one minute, then rinse with water.

420. DRY UP BLEMISHES

- 1 teaspoon (5 mL) lemon juice
- 1 teaspoon (5 mL) rose water

Mix lemon juice and rose water, then dab on blemish with a cotton ball.

421. SOFTEN CORNS

- 1 lemon wedge, cut into smaller pieces
- warm water

Soak feet in warm water for 10 minutes. Apply a small piece of lemon to the corn, then wrap with a bandage and keep on overnight. In the morning, clean and dry the area.

422. TAKE A STRESS-BUSTING BATH

Slice up one or two lemons and float the slices in your bath. Add a few drops of lemon essential oil to create an even more lemon-scented experience. Inhale and exhale deeply and slowly as you relax.

423. LIGHTEN NAILS

- ¼ cup (60 mL) lemon juice
- ¼ cup (60 mL) vinegar
- ¼ cup (60 mL) water

Soak stained fingernails or toenails in the lemon juice for 10 minutes, then rinse. Mix vinegar and water together, then dab on vinegar solution and buff; rinse and moisturize.

424. TAKE A HEALTHFUL MORNING TONIC

- Juice of 6 lemons
- 1 lemon, sliced
- pitcher of ice water

With its antioxidants, vitamin C, bioflavonoids and other healthy components, lemon has been shown to have antiviral, antibacterial, and immune boosting properties. Take advantage of these with a daily lemon tonic. Squeeze the lemon juice into the pitcher of water, add the slices, and keep in the refrigerator. Drink a glass each morning to get your day off to a healthy start.

425. INCREASE CONCENTRATION

Studies show that the invigorating aroma of lemons increases attention and concentration. When you need your mental faculties to be at their strongest, try using an aromatherapy diffuser and a few drops of lemon essential oil to send a gentle lemon scent wafting through your workspace.

426. CALM AND CLEAN WITH A STEAM FACIAL

- 1 large bowl
- 1 large towel
- 4 cups boiling water
- 1 sliced lemon

This steam treatment deep cleans pores while imparting feelings of relaxation and calmness. Place the large bowl on a stable surface and pour in the boiling water. Add lemon slices. Place the towel over your head and the bowl, and hover with your face several inches above the water. Inhale and exhale slowly and deeply for five minutes. When finished, splash face with cold water.

427. INDULGE YOUR FEET

- Juice of half a lemon
- 2 bananas
- 2 tablespoons (30 mL) fine sea salt
- 2 teaspoons (10 mL) grapeseed oil

Slice and mash bananas. Add the lemon juice. Stir in the remaining ingredients and mix until the consistency is a firm mush. Cover your feet with this banana-lemon mash, massage gently, and sit for 10 minutes. Rinse off with warm water, dry thoroughly, and apply moisturizer.

428. SCRUB WITH LEMON SUGAR

- ½ cup (250 mL) granulated sugar, white or brown
- 1 tablespoon (15 mL) finely chopped lemon peel
- 1 tablespoon (15 mL) olive oil

Make a paste. Apply with fingertips or washcloth to body, gently massaging in a circular motion. Rinse off completely. Pat dry and moisturize.

429. FILL A ROOM WITH THE SCENT OF LEMONS

• 3 to 6 lemons

Make dried citrus peels to use in potpourri and give your rooms a fresh lemon scent naturally. To dry the lemons, cut off each end and slice each lemon into thin pieces about ⅛-inch (3 mm) thick. Place slices on a wire rack over a cookie sheet, and bake in oven at low heat for 4 hours, turning once. Remove and let cool. Use the slices whole to make potpourri, adding herbs.

430. STAY WARM WITH LEMONS

A substance found in lemons (and other citrus) called hesperidin has been shown to increase blood flow, and studies are underway to discover whether an extra dose of citrus can actually help you stay warmer in cold temperatures. Add a healthy squeeze of lemon juice to water or tea and see for yourself.

CHAPTER 4

Arts, Crafts, and Science

431. GROW SALT CRYSTALS

- salt
- water
- piece of cardboard

Bring water to a boil, and stir in the salt until no more will dissolve (you will see salt crystals on the bottom of the pan). This is a saturated solution. Remove from heat, and thoroughly soak the cardboard in the saturated saltwater solution. Place the wet cardboard on a cookie sheet or pie plate, and set on a sunny window-sill, then wait—salt crystals will start to form in about 1 to 2 days.

432. MAKE A SALT CRYSTAL STRING

Follow the directions in GROW SALT CRYSTALS on page 174 to make the saturated solution. Pour into a clean glass jar. Tie a piece of string around a toothpick or pencil, and place it over the jar opening so the string dangles into the water. Place the jar on a sunny windowsill and let sit for several days to weeks.

433. SEE HOW SALT AFFECTS FREEZING

This simple experiment shows how salt lowers the temperature at which water freezes. Simply fill 2 paper cups, one with fresh water and the other with a solution of 1 cup (250 mL) water and 1 tablespoon (15 mL) salt. Put both in the freezer and check every 10 minutes to see how long it takes each to freeze.

434. WRITE YOUR NAME IN SALT

- Food coloring
- Non-toxic glue
- Construction or copier paper
- Salt

In individual cups, mix up salt and food coloring to get the desired colors. Use the glue to write your name, then sprinkle or spoon the colored salt onto the glue. Let dry and brush or shake off the extra salt.

435. SET VOTIVES IN SALT

Votive candles

½ cup (250 mL) salt for each votive

wide-mouth clear glass jars or glasses

food coloring (optional)

Color salt to desired shades. Pour salt into jar or glass, and place votive inside.

436. MAKE A SALT CRYSTAL SNOWFLAKE

- Saturated salt solution
- Heavy black cardstock
- Paintbrush
- String

Follow the directions in GROW SALT CRYSTALS on page 174 to make the saturated solution, and pour it into a bowl. Let cool slightly. Dip the paintbrush in the solution use it to paint a snowflake design on the black cardstock. Poke a hole in the top of the paper and string it, then hang in a sunny spot and wait for your crystal snowflake to develop.

437. TEXTURIZE A WATERCOLOR PAINTING

Sprinkle salt on a watercolor while it is still wet, and let dry. It will take on an interesting texture that transforms the painting in a cool way.

438. LIGHT THE WAY WITH SALT LUMINARIES

• 6 empty baby food or other small jars

• 1 cup (250 mL) Epsom salt

• thinned white craft glue

• food coloring

• votive candles

Pour the Epsom salt in a large bowl or paper plate. Mix in one or two drops of food coloring and stir to achieve the color you want. Apply thinned white craft glue to the outside of the jars in a thick, even layer. Roll the jars in the salt so it adheres. Let dry. Place a candle inside.

439. CRAFT SALT DOUGH ORNAMENTS

- 1 cup (250 mL) salt
- 2 cups (500 mL) flour
- 1 cup (250 mL) water

Combine salt and flour in mixer; slowly add water until dough forms. Remove and knead for 5 to 10 minutes until smooth. Roll out dough into a thin sheet, then use cookie cutters to cut shapes. Poke a hole through the dough if you want to string the ornament for hanging. Decorate. Air dry for a week to harden.

440. PAINT WITH SALT

- Construction paper or cardstock
- Non-toxic glue
- Salt
- Food coloring

Use the glue to make a design on the paper. Pour an ample amount of salt over the glue; shake off excess. Dip paintbrush in food coloring and apply to the salt design. Let dry completely before displaying.

441. DISSOLVE AN EGGSHELL

Make a "naked" egg by placing a raw egg, shell on, in a clear glass jar and pouring white vinegar over it to fully cover. After about 12 hours, you should start to see the shell dissolving; by 36 hours, it will likely be gone, leaving only a thin membrane holding the egg.

442. MAKE A LAVA LAMP

- Empty clear plastic bottle with cap
- Vegetable oil
- 4 tablespoons (120 mL) baking soda
- 1 cup (250 mL) white vinegar
- food coloring
- eye dropper

Pour baking soda into bottle and shake to flatten. Slowly pour the oil into the bottle, trying not to disturb the baking soda. Pour the vinegar into a separate bowl, and mix in food coloring. Using the eye dropper, deposit several drops of colored vinegar into the soda bottle and watch the reaction.

443. MAKE YOUR OWN
NON-TOXIC, EDIBLE CRAFT GLUE

- 1 cup (250 mL) flour
- 1 ½ cups (360 mL) water
- ⅓ cup (80 mL) sugar
- 1 teaspoon (5 mL) white vinegar

In a saucepan, mix 1 cup (250 mL) of flour with sugar, then add half the water and mix into a thick paste before adding the rest of the water. Add vinegar and heat on medium until mixture thickens. Pour into a jar with airtight lid. Keep in the refrigerator up to two weeks.

444. MAKE
MULTICOLORED FIZZ

- white vinegar
- baking soda
- food coloring in different shades
- a plastic cup for each color

Put a few shakes of baking soda in each cup, then add food coloring to the cups, either individual colors or in fun combinations. Pour in the vinegar and the cups will foam with color.

445. BLOW UP BALLOONS WITH CHEMISTRY

- ½ cup (120 mL) white vinegar
- ¼ cup (60 mL) baking soda
- 1 balloon
- 1 empty 12 oz. (350 mL) soda bottle

Spoon the baking soda into the balloon. Pour the vinegar into the bottle. Carefully fit the balloon opening over the mouth of the bottle, then tip the balloon so the baking soda flows into the bottle—hold the balloon on firmly. The reaction when the vinegar and baking soda meet will be fast and fizzy, and the resulting carbon dioxide gas will fill the balloon.

446. CLEAN PENNIES

- ¼ cup (60 mL) white vinegar
- 1 teaspoon (5 mL) salt
- dirty pennies
- glass bowl

Pour the vinegar into the bowl and stir in the salt. Put the pennies into the solution and wait 2 minutes. Take out the newly shiny pennies and rinse with water.

447. MAKE BEANS DANCE

- 1 cup (250 mL) water
- 1 tablespoon (15 mL) baking soda
- 1 tablespoon (15 mL) white vinegar
- handful of dried beans
- tall, clear glass

Pour water into glass, follow with baking soda, and drop in beans. Add the vinegar and let the dancing begin.

448. DYE RICE

- 6 cups uncooked rice
- 6 tablespoons (90 mL) white vinegar
- 6 shades of food coloring
- 6 sealable plastic bags

Put 1 cup of rice in each bag. In each of 6 small cups, mix up food coloring with a tablespoon (15 mL) of vinegar. Pour one color vinegar into a bag, seal tightly, and mush it around until all the rice is colored. Spread the colored rice on a sheet of wax paper and dry completely. These brightly colored grains are great for crafting—make a layered jar of colored rice or sprinkle on glue designs to create textured art.

449. MAKE
NATURAL PLASTIC

- 1 cup (250 mL) milk
- 4 teaspoons (20 mL) white vinegar

In a small saucepan, heat milk but do not let it come to a boil. Add vinegar and stir for about a minute—globules will begin to form. Remove from heat and pour through a strainer. Run cool water over the blobs. When they are cool, you can shape them—after a few days the shapes will harden.

450. FLOAT A
BATHTUB BOAT

- 3 tablespoons (45 mL) baking soda
- ¼ cup (120 mL) white vinegar
- empty soda bottle with cap
- 3 toilet paper squares

Do this in the bathtub or kiddie pool. Spoon the baking soda onto the toilet paper squares and fold into individual packets. Poke the packets into the bottle. With the cap in one hand, pour the vinegar into the bottle, and immediately screw on the cap. Place the bottle in the water and watch it move.

451. MAKE A VINEGAR VOLCANO

- ½ cup (120 mL) vinegar
- 2 tablespoons (30 mL) baking soda
- red food coloring
- a few drops dishwashing liquid
- tin foil
- tray for holding the mess

Place the soda bottle on the tray and build a volcano of tin foil around it, keeping the mouth of the bottle clear. (You can also make a volcano from flour or papier mâché.) Pour water into the bottle until it is almost full; add several drops of red food coloring, then a few drops of dishwashing detergent. Spoon in the baking soda, then slowly pour in the vinegar—now watch the volcano erupt.

452. PROVE THAT OIL AND WATER DON'T MIX

- ½ cup (120 mL) olive oil
- ½ cup (120 mL) water
- food coloring
- empty, clear soft drink bottle

Mix food coloring in the water. Pour the olive oil into the bottle. Pour the colored water into the bottle. Shake vigorously, then set it down and observe.

453. MARBELIZE EASTER EGGS

A few drops of olive oil in the egg dye will help give eggs a marbleized effect.

454. MAKE "STAINED GLASS" ART

Use crayons on heavy construction paper to create an image. Dip a cotton ball in olive oil, then gently wipe it over the art for a stained glass effect. Let dry and display.

455. WRITE A SECRET MESSAGE

A solution of equal parts baking soda and water makes an "invisible ink" that can be revealed by exposing it to heat. Use a cotton swab to write a secret note. Once it is completely dry, hold the paper over a source of heat, such as a lightbulb, to reveal the secret message.

456. PAINT THE SIDEWALK

- 1 cup (250 mL) baking soda
- ½ cup (120 mL) cornstarch
- hot water
- food coloring

Mix the baking soda and cornstarch, then stir in the water and food coloring. Repeat for different colors, then use a sponge or wide brush to make sidewalk art that will wash away easily.

457. ADD FIZZ TO SIDEWALK ART

Use the sidewalk paint on page 187 to create a piece of art you'd like to see in bubbles. Spritz the art with white vinegar and watch it fizz.

458. MAKE SCULPTING "CLAY"

- 2 cups (500 mL) baking soda
- 1 cup (250 mL) cornstarch
- 1 ¼ cups (300 mL) cold water
- food coloring (optional)

In a saucepan, stir together baking soda, cornstarch, and water. (If you are adding food coloring, do it now.) Cook over medium heat, stirring constantly for approximately 10 to 15 minutes, until the clay has thickened. Pour into a bowl and cover with a damp cloth. When clay has cooled, it is ready to be shaped. Let sculptures dry overnight to harden.

459. WRITE WITH INVISIBLE INK

- Juice of half a lemon
- ½ teaspoon (3 mL) water

Mix the water and lemon juice with a spoon. Dip a paintbrush into the mixture and write a message on white paper. When it dries, the writing will be invisible. To reveal the secret message, heat the paper by holding it close to a light bulb.

460. DO A LEMONY WATERCOLOR

- 1 lemon, quartered
- watercolor cardstock
- watercolors

Apply several colors until the cardstock is completely painted with a fun design. While the paint is still wet, squeeze a few drops of lemon juice over the painting, wait a minute or two, then dab with a tissue. The result is a lovely faded effect.

461. MAKE
LEMON-SCENTED BUBBLES

- 1 teaspoon (5 mL) baking soda
- Liquid dishwashing soap
- Juice of half a lemon

Pour the baking soda into a clean glass or jar. Add a squeeze of dishwashing soap. Pour in the lemon juice and watch it fizz. When you're done with the experiment, you can use the lemony suds to clean something!

462. GET LEMON POWER

- 1 medium lemon
- 2-inch (5-cm) piece of copper wire
- 2-inch (5-cm) zinc-coated nail
- 4 wires with alligator clips
- small holiday light or LED with 2-inch (5-cm) lead

Roll the lemon on a table several times to soften. Insert the wire and nail into the lemon so they are not touching. Attach the clips to the wire and nail and to the LED, and watch it light up.

463. DRY LEMONS AND STRING THEM

• 4 to 6 lemons, sliced into rounds

• string or yarn

Dry the lemon slices in the oven, then string them into a garland.

464. BRIGHTEN A ROOM WITH A LEMON POMANDER

Particularly nice over the winter holidays, a lemon studded with cloves adds a wonderful scent to any room and looks nice, too. Poke even rows of holes all over your lemon with a knitting needle. Stick whole cloves into the holes, working your way around the lemon until it is completely covered. Rest in a decorative bowl or hang with a ribbon.

465. SCRUB FLOWERPOTS

Clean last year's grubby flowerpots with salt. Pour sea salt into the pot and use a stiff brush to scour the inside of the pot clean.

466. PLANT ROSES

When putting in new rose plants, add a tablespoon (15 mL) of Epsom salt to each hole before planting.

467. SWITCH TO A SALTWATER POOL

If you're building a pool or updating an existing one, consider a saltwater pool instead. You will be exposed to less chlorine, and dissolved salt can cleanse and sanitize water very effectively.

468. BOOST EVERGREENS

For denser, greener foliage, work a tablespoon (15 mL) of Epsom salt into the soil for every 9 square feet (1 square m) every season.

469. WATER VEGETABLES

- 2 tablespoons (30 mL) Epsom salt
- 1 gallon (4 L) water

Dissolve Epsom salt in water then use it to water vegetable gardens once a month. The magnesium and sulfate found in Epsom salt (not any other kind of salt, so don't substitute) can be beneficial to plants.

470. FEED THE TOMATOES

Magnesium can help you grow healthier tomatoes. Work a tablespoon (15 mL) of Epsom salt into the soil before planting. Every 2 to 3 weeks, water with the Espom salt recipe above.

471. KILL WEEDS

Salt is anathema to plants, so use it very selectively. A pinch at the base of a persistent weed will kill it, but if you spread salt around your garden, you will render the soil toxic. Indeed, the ancient practice of "salting the earth" was used to punish conquered lands or render the property of a criminal unusable. Moderation is the key.

472. KILL SLUGS

Salt kills slugs by dehydrating them. You can sprinkle the deadly crystals right onto slugs in your garden.

473. CLEAN UP OIL STAINS

Scrub oil stains on a garage floor with a paste of salt and water.

474. GET RID OF ANTHILLS

To eliminate an anthill without chemicals, pour a full kettle of boiling water over it, and follow with full-strength white vinegar.

475. MAKE YOUR OWN PET DETERRENT SPRAY

Combine equal parts white vinegar and water in a spray bottle. Spray just a bit at pet's nose to dissuade a puppy or kitten from destructive behaviors.

476. TRAIN YOUR PUPPY NOT TO CHEW

To make your favorite household item less appealing as puppy chews, spray it liberally with a formula of 3 parts water to 1 part white vinegar.

477. CLEAN WINDSHIELD WIPER BLADES

Wipe down with full-strength white vinegar.

478. ERADICATE ALL TRACES OF OLD BUMPER STICKERS

Soak a rag in full-strength white vinegar and use it to get rid of bumper stickers. Thoroughly saturate the sticker with the vinegar; let stand 10 minutes, then scrub off.

479. DEODORIZE CAR INTERIORS

Wet a clean cloth with full-strength white vinegar. Lightly wipe it over all the upholstery and mats in your car to help eliminate bad smells.

480. NATURALLY CLEAN PET CAGE FLOORS

Wipe down with full-strength white vinegar.

481. DESTREAK WINDSHIELDS

Wipe down windshields with full-strength white vinegar. It will also dissolve old bird droppings.

482. REPEL MOSQUITOS

Pour full-strength white or apple cider vinegar into a spray bottle—spritz liberally over exposed skin and clothing to keep mosquitos at bay.

483. TEST SOIL FOR ALKALINITY

Dig up a sample of dry soil from your garden, and pour vinegar onto it. If it fizzes, your soil is alkaline (a pH of 7 or higher). Amend it with organic matter, such as pine needle mulch.

484. DETER FLEAS

- 1 tablespoon (15 mL) apple cider vinegar
- 1 gallon (4 L) clean water

This water mixture will not put off your dog but it will deter fleas.

485. TREAT HAIRBALLS

A teaspoon (5 mL) of olive oil in your cat's food may help to prevent hairballs.

486. LUBRICATE CRACKED PAWS

Rub a little olive oil into your dog's cracked paws to help soften and heal the damage.

487. CLEAN UP GARDEN TOOLS

Scrape off the dirt, rinse, and dry. Then condition your garden tools by wiping them down with olive oil. Rinse again and dry. This will help prevent corrosion.

488. RECONDITION PAINT BRUSHES

If paint brushes have become hardened, let them sit with bristles immersed in olive oil for 30 minutes, then wipe clean.

489. SWEETEN A STINKY DOG

In between full shampoos, you can freshen up your dog's coat with a sprinkle of baking soda. Massage it into the dog's fur then brush out thoroughly.

490. ERADICATE EVIDENCE OF PET ACCIDENTS

If it is still wet, sprinkle baking soda over the malodorous spot and scrub clean. If it has dried already and the odor is lingering, prepare a paste of baking soda and water and press it into the spot. Let dry overnight and vacuum up.

491. FRESHEN UP LITTER BOXES

In between changes, liberally sprinkle baking soda over a cleaned-up litter box.

492. CLEAN UP DIRTY PET TOYS

- 3 tablespoons (45 mL) baking soda
- 3 cups (750 mL) warm water

Dissolve baking soda in water. Dip pet toys in the solution and scrub as needed.

493. TEST SOIL FOR ACIDITY

Pour baking soda on a wet soil sample; if it fizzes, your soil is acidic (a pH of less than 7). Adding crushed eggshells to your compost may help.

494. DISCOURAGE PATIO WEEDS

Prevent weeds from growing between pavers or stones by pouring baking soda into the spaces.

495. BATTLE POWDERY MILDEW

- 1 tablespoon (15 mL) baking soda
- 1 tablespoon (15 mL) vegetable oil
- 1 tablespoon (15 mL) liquid soap
- 1 gallon (4 L) water

An all-too-common fungal disease that manifests as white or gray powdery spots, powdery mildew can be both prevented and treated with baking soda. Mix all the ingredients together and pour into a spray bottle; once a week, preferably in the morning, thoroughly spray plants.

496. FIGHT BLACK SPOT

- 4 tablespoons (60 mL) baking soda
- 2 tablespoons (30 mL) horticultural oil
- 1 gallon (4 L) water

Prevent this dreaded fungal disease from marring your roses by spraying roses weekly, ideally in the early part of the day; be sure to get the undersides of the leaves.

497. GROW SWEETER TOMATOES

Many vegetable gardeners find that a sprinkle of baking soda in the soil around tomato plants results in sweeter tomatoes.

498. SMOOTH A WALL

If you need to quickly fill in small dents or nail holes in a wall, and you have no spackle, try baking soda! A thick paste of baking soda and toothpaste can be a good emergency filler.

499. CLEAN HEADLIGHTS

- 1 tablespoon (15 mL) baking soda
- 1 quart (1 L) water

Dissolve the baking soda in the water. Dip a clean rag in the solution and use it to scrub headlights.

500. ELIMINATE GREASY STAINS IN THE GARAGE

Pour baking soda generously on stain; dip a firm-bristled brush in water and use it to scrub away the marks.

501. FRESHEN UP YOUR CAR

Sprinkle baking soda liberally over car seats and floor mats. Let stand overnight then vacuum it up for a fresher smelling car.

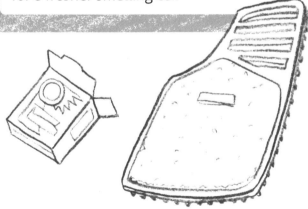

Index

501 AMAZING USES FOR SALT, VINEGAR,
BAKING SODA, OLIVE OIL & LEMONS

The author would like to thank Peter Norton, Lori Asbury, Traci Douglas, and everyone at Thunder Bay Press who helped bring this book to fruition; J. Longo for his terrific design and illustrations; Susan Marcinek and Laura Maiorana for salt and olive oil tips, and all the other household hints mavens whose suggestions found their way into the pages of this book—their resourcefulness and enthusiasm for green living continues to inspire. Any errors are mine alone. –LMW

Laura M. Westdale is a writer and editor who specializes in home and garden topics. She lives in Brooklyn, NY.